STECK-VAUGHN
GED
Writing Skills

EXERCISE BOOK

DONNA D. AMSTUTZ

STECK-VAUGHN ®
C O M P A N Y
ELEMENTARY • SECONDARY • ADULT • LIBRARY

t the Author

Donna D. Amstutz, Ph.D., has been active in adult education for more than twenty years. Dr. Amstutz taught ABE/GED at a community college, became a materials/curriculum specialist for a literacy resource center and conducted staff development for over thirty adult education programs in Illinois. She has developed ABE/GED writing and math curriculum for City Colleges of Chicago and administered their ABE/GED program. Currently Dr. Amstutz is Assistant Professor of Lifelong Learning and Instruction at the University of Wyoming, where she teaches graduate courses in literacy. She is also the Director of the Wyoming Literacy Resource Center, where she continues to provide professional development to adult educators in the western part of the United States.

Staff Credits

Executive Editor:	Ellen Northcutt
Supervising Editor:	Tim Collins
Design Manager:	John J. Harrison
Cover Design:	Rhonda Childress

ISBN 0-8114-7367-8

Copyright © 1996 Steck-Vaughn Company

3 4 5 6 7 8 9 DBH 99 98 97 96

Contents

To the Learner 2

Unit 1: Mechanics 4
Capitalization 4
Comma Use 5
Semicolons and Commas 7
Apostrophes......................... 8
Quotation Marks..................... 9
GED Spelling List................... 10
Spelling Practice 14
GED Practice: Mechanics 16

Unit 2: Usage 20
Subject/Verb Agreement 20
Irregular Verbs 23
Verb Tenses 25
Perfect Tense....................... 26
Commonly Confused Verbs............ 27
GED Practice: Verbs 28
Plural and Possessive Nouns 30
Personal Pronouns 31
Pronoun Antecedents 32
Indefinite Pronoun Antecedents 33
Pronoun Errors 34
Who/Whom 35
Homonyms........................... 36
Adjectives 37
GED Practice: Usage 38

Unit 3: Sentence Structure 42
Sentence Fragments................. 42
Run-On Sentences.................. 43
Sentence Combining 44
Parallel Structure.................. 46
Subordination 47
Sentence Revising.................. 49

GED Practice: Sentence Revising I 52
GED Practice: Sentence Revising II 53
Misplaced Modifiers 54
Dangling Modifiers.................. 55
Unclear Pronoun Reference 56
Pronoun Reference in a Passage 57
GED Practice: Sentence Structure...... 58

Simulated GED Test A............. 62
Analysis of Performance: Writing Skills
  Simulated Test A................. 76

Simulated GED Test B............. 77
Analysis of Performance: Writing Skills
  Simulated Test B................. 91

Answers and Explanations........ 92

Instructions for Evaluating the GED Essay 108

Answer Sheets 109

To the Learner

This exercise book for Part I of the GED Writing Skills Test provides you with the review and practice in answering the types of questions found on the actual GED Writing Skills Test, Part I. Part II of the GED Writing Skills Test, writing an essay, is covered in the *Steck-Vaughn GED: The Essay*.

This workbook can be used along with the *Steck-Vaughn GED Writing Skills* book or the *Steck-Vaughn Complete GED Preparation* book or other appropriate materials. Cross references to these Steck-Vaughn books are supplied for your convenience on exercise pages 4–61 and the correlation chart on the following page. This book contains practice exercises and two full-length simulated GED tests.

Practice Exercises

Part I of the GED Writing Skills Test examines your command of English grammar. The forty-four lessons in this workbook give you practice on a variety of grammar skills. The practice is divided into three units: mechanics, usage, and sentence structure.

Unit 1: Mechanics

The mechanics unit reviews capitalization, punctuation, and spelling. An official master list of spelling words is included for you to review. Read the spelling words carefully, but do not try to memorize too many at a time. Instead, break the list into groups of 10–12. Practice these groups of words as you work through the rest of the book.

Unit 2: Usage

The usage unit gives you practice in subject/verb agreement. Also included are the correct use of verb, noun, adjective, and pronoun forms.

Unit 3: Sentence Structure

The sentence structure unit covers completeness of sentences, parallel structure, subordination, and sentence revising and combining.

Simulated Tests

This workbook contains two complete full-length Simulated GED Writing Skills Practice Tests. Each Simulated Test has the same number of items as the GED Test and provides practice with similar item types as found on the GED Test. The Simulated Tests can help you decide if you are ready to take the GED Writing Skills Test.

To get the most benefit from the Simulated Tests, take each test under the same restrictions as for the actual GED Test. For each test, complete the 55 items in Part I within 75 minutes. Each Simulated Test also contains Part II, an essay topic. Take no more than 45 minutes to complete the essay. Space the two examinations apart by at least a week.

Reading Passages

Periodically throughout the book you will see GED Practice sections. These consist of short reading passages followed by a set of questions. Reading passages also appear in the two full-length Simulated Tests. Remember to read each passage carefully before you begin to answer the questions. Reading the passage carefully and in advance of the questions may help you spot the errors right away.

Question Types

All of the questions on the GED Writing Skills Test, Part I are multiple-choice. There are three types of questions: sentence correction, sentence revision, and construction shift.

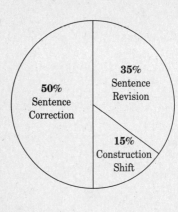

1. Sentence Correction: About 50% of the questions ask you, "What correction should be made to this sentence?" These items test your knowledge of mechanics, usage, and sentence structure.

Example: This is the most commonest cause of malfunctions in household appliances.

2. Sentence Revision: Thirty-five percent of the items are sentence revision. In this question type, a part of a sentence is underlined. You are asked which of five choices is the best way to write the underlined portion. The first answer choice is always the same as the original sentence.

Example: Contrary to popular belief, it <u>do not take</u> much space to grow a few vegetables.

3. Construction Shift: Fifteen percent of the items are construction shifts. These questions ask you the best way to rewrite an entire sentence, or the best way to combine two sentences. The original sentences do not contain errors. The rewritten or combined sentences must retain the meaning of the original sentence(s).

Example: There are other reasons why people are attracted to gardening. The reasons include the convenience of having fresh vegetables and the money saved by growing their own food.

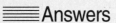

Answers

The answer sections give complete explanations of why an answer is correct, and why the other answer choices are incorrect. Sometimes, by studying the reason an answer is incorrect, you can learn to avoid a similar problem in the future.

Analysis of Performance Charts

After each Simulated Test, an Analysis of Performance Chart will help you determine if you are ready to take Part I of the GED Writing Skills Test. The charts give a breakdown by content area (mechanics, usage, and sentence structure) and by question type (sentence correction, sentence revision, and construction shift). By completing these charts, you can determine your own strengths and weaknesses in the writing skills area.

Correlation Chart

The following chart shows how the sections of this exercise book relate to sections of other Steck-Vaughn GED preparation books. Refer to these two books for further instruction or review.

CONTENT AREAS	Mechanics	Usage	Sentence Structure
BOOK TITLES Steck-Vaughn GED Writing Skills book	Unit 1	Unit 2	Unit 3
Steck-Vaughn GED Writing Skills, Part 1 Exercise Book	Unit 1	Unit 2	Unit 3
Steck-Vaughn Complete GED Preparation book	Unit 1, Mechanics	Unit 1, Usage	Unit 1, Sentence Structure

Unit 1 Mechanics

Capitalization

Review: 1. Capitalize the names of specific people, places, events, and organizations.
   Example: Alice went to see Dr. Jones in the Brown Building.
2. Capitalize the beginning of a sentence in quotation marks.
   Example: I said, "Our softball game starts at noon."
3. Never capitalize the names of seasons.
   Example: We plant a garden in the spring and the fall.
4. Capitalize titles used with a person's name.
   Example: District Judge Wilma Brown will hear the court case.
5. Capitalize directions only when they refer to a specific area of the city, country, or world.
   Example: Florida is part of the South.
6. Capitalize proper adjectives.
   Example: Elena and Charles like Chinese food.

Directions: Circle the word or words that contain capitalization errors in the following sentences. Some sentences are correct as written.
Example: John asked, "(did) your job interview go well?"

1. The reports, detailing the difficulties encountered by terminally ill persons who could not afford insurance, were presented to the Director of the State health agency.

2. Although Tanya had lived in Cleveland for the past twenty years, she originally came from the south.

3. Mr. Pearman, who exercises regularly at the YMCA, called doctor Jackson about the unusual pain in his back.

4. The quality of American cars has increased; as a result, the sale of japanese and german cars has decreased.

5. Florists sell more flowers on Mother's Day than on any other holiday of the year.

6. The Environmental Protection Agency last week declared, "pollution is still threatening the future of America."

7. According to the Constitution, the Federal Government has the power to levy taxes, declare War, and enforce legislation.

8. The number of endangered species in the pacific ocean has generated concern by the Oceanographic Society.

9. Kingston, the capital of jamaica, has suffered a large increase in unemployment due to a reduction in the Tourist trade.

10. After Mrs. Ramirez's son graduated from High School, he worked two years before entering a vocational program at Rock Valley community college.

11. While he was on a fact-finding tour of rural Tennessee, Senator Millikan offered the local citizens a chance to express their views regarding the proposed interstate highway.

12. Television was primarily responsible for making the World aware of the devastating drought in africa during the 1980's.

13. Since the air controller's strike last Spring, many Unions have increased their political activities.

14. I bought some french bread and some italian pastries at the bakery.

15. The candidate for mayor said, "there will be no increase in City taxes or in Utility rates if I'm elected."

Comma Use I

Review: 1. Use a comma to separate more than two items on a list.*
    Example: People reacted to the earthquake with fear, disbelief, anger, and confusion.
2. Use commas to separate a descriptive word or phrase from the noun being described.
    Example: Joan Haskell, my dentist, has been in practice for ten years.
3. Use a comma to separate a part of a sentence that cannot stand alone only when that part comes first.
    Example: When the rain started, we all ran inside the building.
4. Use a comma to separate long introductory phrases from the rest of the sentence.
    Example: Because the symptoms of mononucleosis include feeling tired and achy, it is often confused with the flu.
5. Use a comma between a city and state and after the state.
    Example: Kim Sung will move from Cleveland, Ohio, to Chicago, Illinois.
    *Placement of a comma before <u>and</u> is optional and is not tested on the GED Test. All our examples include the comma.

Directions: Insert commas where needed in the following sentences. Some sentences do not need commas.
Example: John, my neighbor, pays more rent than I do.

1. Volunteers to prepare food package individual meals and deliver food to elderly shut-ins are needed by the Community Action Center.

2. Answering questions regarding nuclear waste the spokesperson for the electric company was visibly nervous.

3. Anthony Ching the union's shop steward provides the company with a list of repairs needed each week to ensure worker safety.

4. The newspaper editor asked the reporter to investigate the accident determine the real cause and identify the person responsible for the damage.

5. Until she had completed the probationary period the new employee was not allowed to use the chemicals alone.

6. To fully understand the situation the dismayed parents asked to speak to the principal.

7. Patients are taught about sound nutrition appropriate exercise and stress reduction.

8. Mrs. Landover the most active club member suggested conducting a bowl-a-thon to raise money.

9. After the job was completed the contractor checked to see if the customers were satisfied.

10. Pittsburgh Pennsylvania is located where the Allegheny and Monongahela rivers come together to form the Ohio River.

11. The list containing the names addresses and phone numbers of each of the applicants was given to the employment office.

12. Jonathan Welch a senator from Texas introduced legislation that would provide stricter punishment for drug pushers.

13. On the way to her job Ms. Chaney drops off her daughter at the Sunshine Child Care Center.

14. Isaac Asimov an award winning scientist also wrote many books.

15. When spring begins many Americans prepare their income tax forms for the Internal Revenue Service.

16. Our summer garden is producing corn squash tomatoes cucumbers and green peppers.

17. Wind insects bats birds moths and butterflies help plants to transfer their pollen from the male to the female plants.

18. Agates semiprecious stones have bands of different colors.

19. Table salt a mineral is found in rocks soil and oceans.

20. Phoenix is the largest city and capital of Arizona.

21. Swimming jogging walking and riding bicycles are all good forms of exercise.

≡ Comma Use II

Review: 1. Do not use commas to set off words that are essential in describing the subject.
Example: The man who wrecked the car had been drinking.
2. Do not use a comma to separate the subject and the verb in the sentence.
Example: My friend from high school met us for dinner.
3. Do not use a comma to separate compound verbs, subjects, or objects within a sentence.
Example: The child screamed and cried when the bee stung her.
4. Never use a comma unless you know a comma use rule for that situation.

Directions: Rewrite the following sentences on another piece of paper, correcting any comma errors. If there are no comma errors, write <u>correct as written</u>.
Example: The clerk who sold me the watch is over there. _____ *correct as written*

1. The vocational component of Dawson Technical Institute offers programs in machine repair data processing and respiratory therapy.

2. The woman, who identified the criminal, was given a reward by the prosecutors.

3. The carpet which they purchased only two years ago was completely ruined by the flood.

4. To comply with state, health regulations people without shoes are not allowed, into most restaurants.

5. Lacemakers, the store that is going out of business, has been a landmark in the downtown area for the past fifty years.

6. The anxious father paced the floor, and talked continuously until his wife delivered the baby.

7. Mr. McArthur a self-made millionaire is a major contributor, to the minority scholarship program.

8. Yesterday the excited bride-to-be bought the invitations addressed the envelopes and deposited them, in the mail.

9. Because of the delay in processing the orders the managers asked the employees to work overtime.

10. The driver of the car, that went speeding through the red light was stopped immediately by the police.

11. Victor recommended by his supervisor was given a promotion to line foreman.

12. Sarah Williams whom I've known for fifteen years was given the Outstanding Adult Student Award, for her commitment to helping others further their education.

13. The runner who was determined to win first place concentrated on his breathing.

14. Wanting to lose weight in order to improve his health Mr. Ferro, contacted several diet programs.

15. When planting flowers, or vegetables always water the ground thoroughly.

16. Citizens who want good leaders must get out to vote in local elections.

17. The car with the sun roof power windows and power locks is the one I want.

18. The passengers and the crew boarded the airplane slowly.

19. Rollerblading, also called inline skating became a popular sport during the 1990s.

20. Knowing how to use a computer, has become an important job skill.

21. Anna's friends took her to lunch, and gave her a cake for her birthday.

22. During their vacation, the Monroes plan to repaint their house plant a garden, and clean out the garage.

23. The man, at the next table, is talking so loudly that we cannot carry on our own conversation.

24. Benjamin's aunt, uncle, and cousin, came to visit him during the holidays.

≡ Semicolons and Commas

Review: 1. Use a comma to join clauses that could stand alone but are joined by the linking words <u>and</u>, <u>but</u>, <u>or</u>, <u>for</u>, and <u>nor</u>.
Example: Let's vote on this plan, and let's take action right away.
2. Use a semicolon to join clauses that can stand alone but are not joined by a linking word.
Example: Our meeting will start at two o'clock; it will be brief.
3. Use a semicolon to separate clauses that could stand alone when there are other commas in the sentence.
Example: We called the police, the fire department, and the emergency medical service; they all responded.
4. Use a semicolon to join two clauses that could stand alone but are joined by the linking words listed below, and always set off this linking word with a comma
Example: We need a new car; however, we don't have enough cash for a down payment.

Linking words

accordingly	moreover	nonetheless	instead	still
for instance	therefore	in fact	besides	then
for example	consequently	however	otherwise	thus
furthermore	nevertheless	indeed	hence	

Directions: Insert the correct punctuation needed in the following sentences.
Example: We went to see a movie, but every seat in the theater was taken.

1. Mrs. Sheared works full-time but she also attends Washington Evening School to prepare for her GED examination.

2. According to management the painters are paid an adequate salary however the painters are continuing to request salary raises.

3. The caseworkers were upset they had just been informed that the child had run away from home again.

4. Many people believe that drunk drivers should have their licenses revoked moreover they believe that drunk drivers who are involved in accidents should go to jail.

5. Doctors urge patients to develop a healthier diet and they encourage regular exercise to strengthen the heart muscle.

6. The number of African American Hispanic and Asian minorities is growing in fact by the year 2010 almost 40 percent of the population under 18 will be minority.

7. The unpopular candidate tried to address the key issues in the campaign but the angry crowd kept interrupting his speech.

8. Discrimination based on gender has been made illegal however many women proclaim that it still exists.

9. The phone customers were enraged the long distance call rate was being increased again.

10. Only 15 percent of court-ordered child support is ever paid by fathers consequently many children are not receiving adequate support.

11. Let's stop at that new restaurant I'm starving.

12. The Andersons must leave at 6:00 A.M. otherwise they will miss their flight to Los Angeles.

13. The American Heart Association urges middle-aged men to get cholesterol screenings and they suggest a low-fat diet to lower a high cholesterol level.

14. Marilyn can return to school next semester or she can look for a job.

15. His hobby is gardening her hobby is playing the piano.

▤▤Apostrophes

Review: 1. Use apostrophes in contractions to take the place of missing letters.
   Example: She won't drive, so I'll do it.
2. Use apostrophes to show possession.
   Example: My daughter's glasses are broken.

Directions: Insert apostrophes in the following sentences where needed. Some sentences do not need apostrophes.
Example: Ten students put test papers on the teacher's desk.

1. The furniture store owner refused to cancel the buyers contract so now he'll have to pay for all that furniture.

2. The suspects fingerprints will be checked against the computer fingerprint division at FBI headquarters to determine if she has a prior record.

3. Floridas residents are generally older than residents in the other forty-nine states.

4. NASA has decided to stop production of its super missiles since the missiles fuel tanks were found to be dangerous.

5. Local school systems have to pay for their drivers training.

6. The woman, denying any wrongdoing, insisted that the jewels were hers.

7. The judge replied that he couldnt preside at the childrens hearing.

8. Unfortunately, the firefighters werent able to control the flames, and the fire spread to nearby buildings.

9. Evidently, the cars exhaust pipes hadnt been working properly for at least three weeks.

10. The task force released its report to the city council members.

11. Although evidence was found that the man was innocent, its unclear why he was in the apartment.

12. Franks automobile wont start when the temperature is below zero.

13. The Congress strongly disapproved of the Presidents solution to the arms race.

14. The foreign visitors were surprised by Chicagos windy weather.

15. The court reporters missing notes were later found on her desk.

16. The familys vacation to the Wisconsin Dells scenic gorge wasnt very expensive.

17. It isnt always easy to spot deceptive advertising, but if the offer sounds too good to be true, it probably is.

18. Were feeding our neighbors dog for a week while they are out of town.

19. The oil companys responsibility for the Valdez, Alaska, oil cleanup should continue as long as oil remains on the beaches.

20. Michael Jackson didnt want his sister LaToya to write a kiss-and-tell book about their family, but LaToya said, "I ll make sure the book is published."

21. My husband promised hed call, but the phone didnt ring and Ive been in the house.

22. In 1989 President Bush called for the American space program to go to Mars, but money will be the plans biggest problem.

23. Hasnt the city council recently voted to add more police officers?

24. Mr. and Mrs. Ray always considered their two sons needs before their own.

25. My sister often says, "Youre going to be sorry if you do that."

26. Many famous people dont like to be bothered by reporters or fans.

27. One of New York Citys biggest attractions is the Statue of Liberty.

28. Cities and counties are the most common forms of local government in the United States.

Quotation Marks

Review: 1. Quotations are used to set off someone's exact words. Generally, commas and other punctuation marks are placed inside the second quotation mark. A comma is also used to introduce a quotation.

Example: "It's time for you children to go to bed," said Mother.

2. If the phrase identifying the speaker interrupts the quotation, set off that phrase with commas. The first comma is placed inside the quotation marks.

Example: "I can always tell," her husband said, "when you're worried about something."

Directions: Insert quotation marks and commas in the following sentences where needed. Some sentences are correct as written.

Example: I said, "It's very nice to meet you."

1. The mayor's aide reported, Mayor Stillwater has appointed an interim director to fill the vacancy caused by Ms. Terrell's resignation.

2. The hotel manager announced, There will be a complimentary dinner for those guests who were disturbed by the noise.

3. The lottery winner screamed, I can't believe I won!

4. Although you can't say that stress directly causes people to be ill said the health counselor stress does significantly affect a person's general health.

5. When the tenants band together to protest unsanitary living conditions, the landlords are more easily persuaded to make improvements explained the lawyer.

6. At an international meeting to support a ban on ozone-destroying chemicals, the concerned representative noted The Earth's ozone helps filter the sun's ultraviolet rays that cause skin cancer. Without it, we would all die.

7. Speaking about a proposed law to ban pornography, the activist said We are drowning in garbage, and this law is a long overdue lifeline.

8. An unemployment specialist reported Low pay is the top reason that millions of one-worker households are poor.

9. Eat plenty of fruit and vegetables said the dietician if you want to be sure you have enough vitamins in your diet.

10. You'll always be welcome here whispered Leon's brother and you don't need an invitation.

11. We provide the best service claimed the car dealer and can arrange financing for almost anyone.

12. Former Detroit mayor Coleman Young once told reporters One thing you learn as mayor is how long it takes to get something done; you have to stay on it.

13. When asked how soon Americans will have smart credit cards, the expert advised Not right away; it's expensive to put the computer terminals in stores that accept the cards.

14. If you wouldn't give your baby a bottle of gin the day after birth, why give it one the day before? asked the doctor who advised pregnant mothers against drinking alcohol.

15. Inpatient mental hospitalization of teenagers has increased dramatically said the doctor to the audience of concerned parents.

16. Whether Pete Rose gambles on the baseball field is his own business said my brother, but I replied No, because he's a public figure that kids look up to, it's everyone's business.

17. Research has shown, said the biologist, that Britain's 5 million house cats kill over 20 million birds a year.

18. Explaining why customers received monthly bills exceeding $10,000, the company spokesperson said The computer had a malfunction in the program that prepares the bills.

GED Spelling List

Master List of Frequently Misspelled Words

The words below are often found on standardized tests. Letters that people often misspell are underlined for you. Use these steps to study the list.

1. Pretest—Ask someone to read each word to you and use the word in a sentence. Write each word on your paper. Then check to see if you've spelled the word correctly. Put an X in the box if you spelled the word correctly.

2. Study List—Make a list of the words you misspelled. Study 10–12 at a time. Underline the letters you have trouble spelling. Practice writing the words.

3. Post-Test—Have someone read to you each list of 10–12 words that you studied. Write the words again and check your work.

a lot	☐	agree	☐	arrange	☐	board	☐
ability	☐	aisle	☐	arrangement	☐	bored	☐
absence	☐	all right	☐	article	☐	borrow	☐
absent	☐	almost	☐	artificial	☐	bottle	☐
abundance	☐	already	☐	ascend	☐	bottom	☐
accept	☐	although	☐	assistance	☐	boundary	☐
acceptable	☐	altogether	☐	assistant	☐	brake	☐
accident	☐	always	☐	associate	☐	breadth	☐
accommodate	☐	amateur	☐	association	☐	breath	☐
accompanied	☐	American	☐	attempt	☐	breathe	☐
accomplish	☐	among	☐	attendance	☐	brilliant	☐
accumulation	☐	amount	☐	attention	☐	building	☐
accuse	☐	analysis	☐	audience	☐	bulletin	☐
accustomed	☐	analyze	☐	August	☐	bureau	☐
ache	☐	angel	☐	author	☐	burial	☐
achieve	☐	angle	☐	automobile	☐	buried	☐
achievement	☐	annual	☐	autumn	☐	bury	☐
acknowledge	☐	another	☐	auxiliary	☐	bushes	☐
acquaintance	☐	answer	☐	available	☐	business	☐
acquainted	☐	antiseptic	☐	avenue	☐		
acquire	☐	anxious	☐	awful	☐	cafeteria	☐
address	☐	apologize	☐	awkward	☐	calculator	☐
addressed	☐	apparatus	☐			calendar	☐
adequate	☐	apparent	☐	bachelor	☐	campaign	☐
advantageous	☐	appear	☐	balance	☐	capital	☐
advantage	☐	appearance	☐	balloon	☐	capitol	☐
advertise	☐	appetite	☐	bargain	☐	captain	☐
advertisement	☐	apply	☐	basic	☐	career	☐
advice	☐	appreciate	☐	beautiful	☐	careful	☐
advisable	☐	appreciation	☐	because	☐	careless	☐
advise	☐	approach	☐	become	☐	carriage	☐
advisor	☐	appropriate	☐	before	☐	carrying	☐
aerial	☐	approval	☐	beginning	☐	category	☐
affect	☐	approve	☐	being	☐	ceiling	☐
affectionate	☐	approximate	☐	believe	☐	cemetery	☐
again	☐	argue	☐	benefit	☐	cereal	☐
against	☐	arguing	☐	benefited	☐	certain	☐
aggravate	☐	argument	☐	between	☐	changeable	☐
aggressive	☐	arouse	☐	bicycle	☐	characteristic	☐

charity ☐	council ☐	disapproval ☐	examine ☐
chief ☐	counsel ☐	disapprove ☐	exceed ☐
choose ☐	counselor ☐	disastrous ☐	excellent ☐
chose ☐	courage ☐	discipline ☐	except ☐
cigarette ☐	courageous ☐	discover ☐	exceptional ☐
circumstance ☐	course ☐	discriminate ☐	exercise ☐
citizen ☐	courteous ☐	disease ☐	exhausted ☐
clothes ☐	courtesy ☐	dissatisfied ☐	exhaustion ☐
clothing ☐	criticism ☐	dissection ☐	exhilaration ☐
coarse ☐	criticize ☐	dissipate ☐	existence ☐
coffee ☐	crystal ☐	distance ☐	exorbitant ☐
collect ☐	curiosity ☐	distinction ☐	expense ☐
college ☐	cylinder ☐	division ☐	experience ☐
column ☐		doctor ☐	experiment ☐
comedy ☐	daily ☐	dollar ☐	explanation ☐
comfortable ☐	daughter ☐	doubt ☐	extreme ☐
commitment ☐	daybreak ☐	dozen ☐	
committed ☐	death ☐		facility ☐
committee ☐	deceive ☐	earnest ☐	factory ☐
communicate ☐	December ☐	easy ☐	familiar ☐
company ☐	deception ☐	ecstasy ☐	fascinate ☐
comparative ☐	decide ☐	ecstatic ☐	fascinating ☐
compel ☐	decision ☐	education ☐	fatigue ☐
competent ☐	decisive ☐	effect ☐	February ☐
competition ☐	deed ☐	efficiency ☐	financial ☐
compliment ☐	definite ☐	efficient ☐	financier ☐
conceal ☐	delicious ☐	eight ☐	flourish ☐
conceit ☐	dependent ☐	either ☐	forcibly ☐
conceivable ☐	deposit ☐	eligibility ☐	forehead ☐
conceive ☐	derelict ☐	eligible ☐	foreign ☐
concentration ☐	descend ☐	eliminate ☐	formal ☐
conception ☐	descent ☐	embarrass ☐	former ☐
condition ☐	describe ☐	embarrassment ☐	fortunate ☐
conference ☐	description ☐	emergency ☐	fourteen ☐
confident ☐	desert ☐	emphasis ☐	fourth ☐
congratulate ☐	desirable ☐	emphasize ☐	frequent ☐
conquer ☐	despair ☐	enclosure ☐	friend ☐
conscience ☐	desperate ☐	encouraging ☐	frightening ☐
conscientious ☐	dessert ☐	endeavor ☐	fundamental ☐
conscious ☐	destruction ☐	engineer ☐	further ☐
consequence ☐	determine ☐	English ☐	
consequently ☐	develop ☐	enormous ☐	gallon ☐
considerable ☐	development ☐	enough ☐	garden ☐
consistency ☐	device ☐	entrance ☐	gardener ☐
consistent ☐	dictator ☐	envelope ☐	general ☐
continual ☐	died ☐	environment ☐	genius ☐
continuous ☐	difference ☐	equipment ☐	government ☐
controlled ☐	different ☐	equipped ☐	governor ☐
controversy ☐	dilemma ☐	especially ☐	grammar ☐
convenience ☐	dinner ☐	essential ☐	grateful ☐
convenient ☐	direction ☐	evening ☐	great ☐
conversation ☐	disappear ☐	evident ☐	grievance ☐
corporal ☐	disappoint ☐	exaggerate ☐	grievous ☐
corroborate ☐	disappointment ☐	exaggeration ☐	grocery ☐
			guarantee ☐

guard ☐
guess ☐
guidance ☐

half ☐
hammer ☐
handkerchief ☐
happiness ☐
healthy ☐
heard ☐
heavy ☐
height ☐
heroes ☐
heroine ☐
hideous ☐
himself ☐
hoarse ☐
holiday ☐
hopeless ☐
hospital ☐
humorous ☐
hurried ☐
hurrying ☐

ignorance ☐
imaginary ☐
imbecile ☐
imitation ☐
immediately ☐
immigrant ☐
incidental ☐
increase ☐
independence ☐
independent ☐
indispensable ☐
inevitable ☐
influence ☐
influential ☐
initiate ☐
innocence ☐
inoculate ☐
inquiry ☐
insistent ☐
instead ☐
instinct ☐
integrity ☐
intellectual ☐
intelligence ☐
intercede ☐
interest ☐
interfere ☐
interference ☐
interpreted ☐
interrupt ☐
invitation ☐

irrelevant ☐
irresistible ☐
irritable ☐
island ☐
its ☐
it's ☐
itself ☐

January ☐
jealous ☐
judgment ☐
journal ☐

kindergarten ☐
kitchen ☐
knew ☐
knock ☐
know ☐
knowledge ☐

labor ☐
laboratory ☐
laid ☐
language ☐
later ☐
latter ☐
laugh ☐
leisure ☐
length ☐
lesson ☐
library ☐
license ☐
light ☐
lightning ☐
likelihood ☐
loose ☐
lose ☐
losing ☐
loyal ☐
loyalty ☐

magazine ☐
maintenance ☐
maneuver ☐
marriage ☐
married ☐
marry ☐
match ☐
material ☐
mathematics ☐
measure ☐
medicine ☐
million ☐
miniature ☐
minimum ☐
miracle ☐

miscellaneous ☐
mischief ☐
mischievous ☐
misspelled ☐
mistake ☐
momentous ☐
monkey ☐
monotonous ☐
moral ☐
morale ☐
mortgage ☐
mountain ☐
mournful ☐
muscle ☐
mysterious ☐
mystery ☐

narrative ☐
natural ☐
necessary ☐
needle ☐
negligence ☐
neighbor ☐
neither ☐
newspaper ☐
newsstand ☐
niece ☐
noticeable ☐

o'clock ☐
obedient ☐
obstacle ☐
occasion ☐
occasional ☐
occur ☐
occurred ☐
occurrence ☐
ocean ☐
offer ☐
often ☐
omission ☐
omit ☐
once ☐
operate ☐
opinion ☐
opportune ☐
opportunity ☐
optimist ☐
optimistic ☐
origin ☐
original ☐
oscillate ☐
ought ☐
ounce ☐
overcoat ☐

paid ☐
pamphlet ☐
panicky ☐
parallel ☐
parallelism ☐
particular ☐
partner ☐
pastime ☐
patience ☐
peace ☐
peaceable ☐
pear ☐
peculiar ☐
pencil ☐
people ☐
perceive ☐
perception ☐
perfect ☐
perform ☐
performance ☐
perhaps ☐
period ☐
permanence ☐
permanent ☐
perpendicular ☐
perseverance ☐
persevere ☐
persistent ☐
persuade ☐
personality ☐
personal ☐
personnel ☐
persuade ☐
persuasion ☐
pertain ☐
picture ☐
piece ☐
plain ☐
playwright ☐
pleasant ☐
please ☐
pleasure ☐
pocket ☐
poison ☐
policeman ☐
political ☐
population ☐
portrayal ☐
positive ☐
possess ☐
possession ☐
possessive ☐
possible ☐
post office ☐

potatoes ☐	receive ☐	signal ☐	through ☐
practical ☐	recipe ☐	significance ☐	title ☐
prairie ☐	recognize ☐	significant ☐	together ☐
precede ☐	recommend ☐	similar ☐	tomorrow ☐
preceding ☐	recuperate ☐	similarity ☐	tongue ☐
precise ☐	referred ☐	sincerely ☐	toward ☐
predictable ☐	rehearsal ☐	site ☐	tragedy ☐
prefer ☐	reign ☐	soldier ☐	transferred ☐
preference ☐	relevant ☐	solemn ☐	treasury ☐
preferential ☐	relieve ☐	sophomore ☐	tremendous ☐
preferred ☐	remedy ☐	soul ☐	tries ☐
prejudice ☐	renovate ☐	source ☐	truly ☐
preparation ☐	repeat ☐	souvenir ☐	twelfth ☐
prepare ☐	repetition ☐	special ☐	twelve ☐
prescription ☐	representative ☐	specified ☐	tyranny ☐
presence ☐	requirements ☐	specimen ☐	
president ☐	resemblance ☐	speech ☐	undoubtedly ☐
prevalent ☐	resistance ☐	stationary ☐	United States ☐
primitive ☐	resource ☐	stationery ☐	university ☐
principal ☐	respectability ☐	statue ☐	unnecessary ☐
principle ☐	responsibility ☐	stockings ☐	unusual ☐
privilege ☐	restaurant ☐	stomach ☐	useful ☐
probably ☐	rhythm ☐	straight ☐	usual ☐
procedure ☐	rhythmical ☐	strength ☐	
proceed ☐	ridiculous ☐	strenuous ☐	vacuum ☐
produce ☐	right ☐	stretch ☐	valley ☐
professional ☐	role ☐	striking ☐	valuable ☐
professor ☐	roll ☐	studying ☐	variety ☐
profitable ☐	roommate ☐	substantial ☐	vegetable ☐
prominent ☐		succeed ☐	vein ☐
promise ☐	sandwich ☐	successful ☐	vengeance ☐
pronounce ☐	Saturday ☐	sudden ☐	versatile ☐
pronunciation ☐	scarcely ☐	superintendent ☐	vicinity ☐
propeller ☐	scene ☐	suppress ☐	vicious ☐
prophet ☐	schedule ☐	surely ☐	view ☐
prospect ☐	science ☐	surprise ☐	village ☐
psychology ☐	scientific ☐	suspense ☐	villain ☐
pursue ☐	scissors ☐	sweat ☐	visitor ☐
pursuit ☐	season ☐	sweet ☐	voice ☐
	secretary ☐	syllable ☐	volume ☐
quality ☐	seize ☐	symmetrical ☐	
quantity ☐	seminar ☐	sympathy ☐	waist ☐
quarreling ☐	sense ☐	synonym ☐	weak ☐
quart ☐	separate ☐		wear ☐
quarter ☐	service ☐	technical ☐	weather ☐
quiet ☐	several ☐	telegram ☐	Wednesday ☐
quite ☐	severely ☐	telephone ☐	week ☐
	shepherd ☐	temperament ☐	weigh ☐
raise ☐	sheriff ☐	temperature ☐	weird ☐
realistic ☐	shining ☐	tenant ☐	whether ☐
realize ☐	shoulder ☐	tendency ☐	which ☐
reason ☐	shriek ☐	tenement ☐	while ☐
rebellion ☐	siege ☐	therefore ☐	whole ☐
recede ☐	sight ☐	thorough ☐	wholly ☐
receipt ☐			whose ☐
			wretched ☐

≣ Spelling Practice I

Review: Homonyms are words that sound alike but that are spelled differently and are different in meaning.

        Example: <u>Their</u> books are over <u>there</u>.

Directions: Circle the misspelled word in each of the following sentences. Write the correct spelling in the blank. Some sentences are correct as written. Write <u>C</u> in the blank before the sentence if it is correct.

Example: _____*their*_____ The men are looking for (there) coats.

_____ 1. The sight for the proposed shopping mall has not been finalized.

_____ 2. The jury couldn't decide weather to believe the victim or the accused criminal.

_____ 3. To apply for the newly created positions, contact the personal office.

_____ 4. The pilot of the plane carefully drove through the thunderstorm.

_____ 5. It was unclear what roll the new assistant to the president would play.

_____ 6. There is a grate fondness between the artist and her promising student.

_____ 7. The auto mechanic for the police department vehicles was concerned about the car's breaks.

_____ 8. Ms. Barker excepted the new position even though it required her to be away from home for several days each month.

_____ 9. It was to the principle's credit that the scores of many students improved this year.

_____ 10. The surgeon removed the vein that had been causing the problem in Rosa's leg.

_____ 11. After working all weak, most people try to take part in some relaxing or enjoyable activities.

_____ 12. The famous pear of dancers performed at the newly renovated theater.

_____ 13. An ambulance was dispatched to the seen of the accident as soon as the report had been called in.

_____ 14. For many years, leaders have discussed how to achieve and maintain world piece.

_____ 15. The internationally known chef used brandy in his favorite dessert.

_____ 16. Every worker new that safety was a top priority in the factory.

_____ 17. Vegetarians don't eat meet, but some do eat fish.

_____ 18. Their is a new restaurant opening on Sixth Street.

Spelling Practice II

Review: 1. Use i before e except after c, or when sounded as a, as in neighbor and weigh.
      Example: My friend received the package.
     2. In words that end in e, drop the final e before adding a suffix that starts with a vowel.
      Example: The lining of my coat is coming out.

Directions: Circle the misspelled word in each group and write the correctly spelled word in the blank. If all the words are correct, write correct.

Example: a store (reciept)
       a hot check
       a good friend

    receipt

1. a deceptive ad
   delicious desert
   the major emphasis

   _____

2. appropriate education
   great oportunity
   decrease in volume

   _____

3. the govenor's daughter
   a special explanation
   a quiet island

   _____

4. dissatisfied customer
   unfair criticism
   fundemental right

   _____

5. the vicious mob
   an outstanding performance
   a peice of bread

   _____

6. the approximate time
   a permenent resident
   the moral of the story

   _____

7. pleasant personality
   significant accomplishment
   political campaign

   _____

8. a pleasurable experience
   the aching mucscle
   January's weather

   _____

9. his telephone manner
   a practicle solution
   neither of the captains

   _____

10. her humorous remedy
    the tremendous tragedy
    a variety of choices

    _____

11. believe to be true
    profitable buisness
    a technical description

    _____

12. a medical prescription
    an emergency situation
    formal approvel

    _____

13. a further thought
    to try again
    a new developement

    _____

14. to recieve permission
    especially easy
    a tape measure

    _____

 **Mechanics**

Directions: Choose the <u>best answer</u> for each item.

Items 1–10 refer to the following paragraph.

(1) Nearly everyone has an ocassional problem falling asleep; many people suffer chronically. (2) Insomnia, once thought to be psychological is now believed to have physical causes. (3) Physical causes of insomnia include pain; use of nasal decongestants, and drinking too much alcohol. (4) Doctors recomend several actions for people who suffer from insomnia. (5) These steps include exercising vigorously avoiding daytime naps, and relaxing before bed. (6) Hypnosis also has been used with success. (7) No specialist on sleeping disorders recommends long-term use of sleeping pills. (8) Pills only mask whatever problem is causing sleeplessness and are potentially addicting. (9) Pills also decrease the quality of sleep, by not allowing the body to sink into deep sleep levels. (10) There are differant levels of sleep that everyone needs to go through each time we fall asleep. (11) One level is called REM, or rapid eye movement, sleep. (12) This is the dreaming level, and a person's eyes move behind closed eyelids as if they were watching a movie. (13) Insomnia may be bothersome, but it can be cured, with patience.

1. Sentence 1: **Nearly everyone has an ocassional problem falling asleep; many people suffer chronically.**

   What correction should be made to this sentence?

   (1) replace <u>everyone</u> with <u>Everyone</u>
   (2) change the spelling of <u>ocassional</u> to <u>occasional</u>
   (3) remove the semicolon after <u>asleep</u>
   (4) insert a comma after <u>suffer</u>
   (5) no correction is necessary

2. Sentence 2: **Insomnia, once thought to be psychological is now believed to have physical causes.**

   What correction should be made to this sentence?

   (1) remove the comma after <u>Insomnia</u>
   (2) insert a comma after <u>psychological</u>
   (3) change the spelling of <u>believed</u> to <u>beleived</u>
   (4) insert a comma after <u>believed</u>
   (5) no correction is necessary

3. Sentence 3: **Physical causes of insomnia include pain; use of nasal decongestants, and drinking too much alcohol.**

   Which of the following is the best way to write the underlined portion of this sentence? If you think the original is the best way, choose option (1).

   (1) include pain; use of
   (2) include pain, use of;
   (3) include, pain, and use of
   (4) include pain, use of
   (5) including pain, and the use of

4. Sentence 4: **Doctors recomend several actions for people who suffer from insomnia.**

   What correction should be made to this sentence?

   (1) change the spelling of <u>recomend</u> to <u>recommend</u>
   (2) change the spelling of <u>several</u> to <u>severel</u>
   (3) insert a comma after <u>actions</u>
   (4) insert a comma after <u>suffer</u>
   (5) no correction is necessary

5. Sentence 5: **These steps include exercising vigorously avoiding daytime naps, and relaxing before bed.**

   Which of the following is the best way to write the underlined portion of this sentence? If you think the original is the best way, choose option (1).

   (1) exercising vigorously avoiding
   (2) exercising vigorously, avoiding
   (3) exercising vigorously; avoiding
   (4) to exercise vigorously avoiding,
   (5) exercising vigorously. Avoiding

6. Sentence 7: **No specailist on sleeping disorders recommends long-term use of sleeping pills.**

   What correction should be made to this sentence?

   (1) change the spelling of specailist to specialist
   (2) insert a semicolon after disorders
   (3) insert a comma after recommends
   (4) insert a comma after use
   (5) no correction is necessary

7. Sentence 8: **Pills only mask whatever problem is causing sleeplessness and are potentially addicting.**

   What correction should be made to this sentence?

   (1) insert a comma after sleeplessness
   (2) replace are with is
   (3) change the spelling of potentially to potentialy
   (4) insert a semicolon after sleeplessness
   (5) no correction is necessary

8. Sentence 9: **Pills also decrease the quality of sleep, by not allowing the body to sink into deep sleep levels.**

   Which of the following is the best way to write the underlined portion of this sentence? If you think the original is the best way, choose option (1).

   (1) sleep, by not allowing
   (2) sleep. by not allowing
   (3) sleep by not allowing
   (4) sleep but do not allow
   (5) sleep, but do not allow

9. Sentence 10: **There are differant levels of sleep that everyone needs to go through each time we fall asleep.**

   What correction should be made to this sentence?

   (1) change the spelling of differant to different.
   (2) insert a comma after levels
   (3) replace everyone with Everyone
   (4) change the spelling of through to thruogh
   (5) no correction is necessary

10. Sentence 13: **Insomnia may be bothersome, but it can be cured, with patience.**

    What correction should be made to this sentence?

    (1) remove the comma after bothersome
    (2) replace the comma after bothersome with a semicolon
    (3) remove the comma after cured
    (4) change the spelling of patience to patiance
    (5) no correction is necessary.

Items 11–22 refer to the following paragraph.

(1) California's redwood trees the tallest living things on earth, stand over 300 feet tall. (2) Some of them were young sprouts' when the Vikings sailed to America. (3) Redwood trees are also known as sequoias or giant sequoias. (4) Redwoods covered vast areas of our planet 30 Million years ago. (5) Now they can only be found along the west Coast. (6) Numerous preserves have been established to save most of the survivors. (7) The shade provided by the huge trees encourages mosses, and ferns to grow at their base. (8) The Redwood National park, at the northern end of California, attracts many visitors each summer. (9) The tourists arrive by bus; but they must walk the last steep 1.4 miles. (10) The parks terrain includes huge granite mountains and deep canyons. (11) Many of the tourists come back year after year, to view the beautiful trees. (12) One tree in particuler, the General Sherman Tree, is estimated to be one of the oldest living things on Earth. (13) Scientists believe "this tree, which is 36.5 feet in diameter, is more than 3,500 years old." (14) In California, laws have been passed to protect the redwoods; and preserve their beauty for future generations.

11. Sentence 1: **California's redwood trees the tallest living things on earth, stand over 300 feet tall.**

    What correction should be made to this sentence?

    (1) replace California's with Californias
    (2) insert a comma after trees
    (3) insert a comma after things
    (4) remove the comma after earth
    (5) no correction is necessary

12. Sentence 2: **Some of them were young sprouts' when the Vikings sailed to America.**

    What correction should be made to this sentence?

    (1) insert a comma after them
    (2) replace sprouts' with sprouts
    (3) insert a comma after sprouts'
    (4) replace Vikings with vikings
    (5) no correction is necessary

13. Sentence 4: **Redwoods covered vast areas of our planet 30 Million years ago.**

    What correction should be made to this sentence?

    (1) replace Redwoods with Redwood's
    (2) insert a comma after areas
    (3) insert a comma after planet
    (4) replace Million with million
    (5) no correction is necessary

14. Sentence 5: **Now they can only be found along the west Coast.**

    What correction should be made to this sentence?

    (1) insert a comma after Now
    (2) insert a semicolon after found
    (3) replace west with West
    (4) replace Coast with coast
    (5) no correction is necessary

15. Sentence 6: **Numerous preserves have been established to save most of the survivors.**

    What correction should be made to this sentence?

    (1) replace preserves with preserves'
    (2) change the spelling of established to establishhed
    (3) insert a comma after established
    (4) replace survivors with Survivors
    (5) no correction is necessary

16. Sentence 7: **The shade provided by the huge trees encourages mosses, and ferns to grow at their base.**

    What correction should be made to this sentence?

    (1) insert a comma after shade
    (2) change the spelling of encourages to encoaruages
    (3) remove the comma after mosses
    (4) insert a comma after grow
    (5) no correction is necessary

17. Sentence 8: **The Redwood National park, at the northern end of California, attracts many visitors each summer.**

    What correction should be made to this sentence?

    (1) replace park with Park
    (2) replace northern with Northern
    (3) remove the comma after California
    (4) change the spelling of visitors to visiters
    (5) no correction is necessary

18. Sentence 9: **The tourists arrive by bus; but they must walk the last steep 1.4 miles.**

    Which of the following is the best way to write the underlined portion of this sentence? If you think the original is the best way, choose option (1).

    (1) by bus; but
    (2) by bus, but
    (3) by bus; but,
    (4) by, bus but
    (5) by bus, but,

19. Sentence 10: **The parks terrain includes huge granite mountains and deep canyons.**

    What correction should be made to this sentence?

    (1) replace parks with park's
    (2) replace parks with Parks
    (3) insert a comma after terrain
    (4) insert a comma after mountains
    (5) no correction is necessary

20. Sentence 11: **Many of the tourists come back year after year, to view the beautiful trees.**

    What correction should be made to this sentence?

    (1) insert a comma after tourists
    (2) insert a semicolon after back
    (3) remove the comma after year
    (4) change the spelling of beautiful to beuatiful
    (5) no correction is necessary

21. Sentence 12: **One tree in particuler, the General Sherman Tree, is estimated to be one of the oldest living things on Earth.**

    What correction should be made to this sentence?

    (1) replace particuler with particular
    (2) remove the comma after particuler
    (3) remove the comma after Tree
    (4) insert a semicolon after be
    (5) no correction is necessary

22. Sentence 13: **Scientists believe "this tree, which is 36.5 feet in diameter, is more than 3,500 years old."**

    What correction should be made to this sentence?

    (1) change the spelling of Scientists to Sceintists
    (2) change the spelling of believe to beleive
    (3) remove the quotation marks
    (4) remove the comma after tree
    (5) no correction is necessary

23. Sentence 14: **In California, laws have been passed to protect the redwoods; and preserve their beauty for future generations.**

    Which of the following is the best way to write the underlined portion of this sentence? If you think the original is the best way, choose option (1).

    (1) redwoods; and preserve
    (2) redwoods and preserve
    (3) redwoods, and preserve
    (4) redwoods; and, preserve
    (5) redwoods, and, preserve

Unit 2 Usage

Subject/Verb Agreement I

Review: 1. Identify the subject of a sentence. The subject tells <u>who</u> or <u>what</u>. Decide if the subject is singular or plural. Use a singular verb with a singular subject and a plural verb with a plural subject.
Examples: This movie <u>is</u> exciting. Those movies <u>are</u> rated PG.
2. Singular verbs end in <u>s</u> or <u>es</u>.
Examples: He <u>has</u> agreed to the terms. He <u>agrees</u> to the terms.
3. Plural verbs do not end in <u>s</u>.
Examples: They <u>have agreed</u> to the terms. They <u>agree</u> to the terms.
4. When the subject is <u>I</u> or <u>You</u>, use a plural verb.
Examples: I <u>agree</u> to the terms. You <u>agree</u> to the terms.

Directions: Circle the correct verb form in each sentence.
Example: You can ((pay), pays) by the month.

1. According to the public defender, everything (has, have) been discussed relative to the plea bargain agreement.

2. The accident victims (was, were) taken to St. Anthony's Hospital in Rockford.

3. The committee (has, have) been discussing the possibility of meeting bimonthly.

4. High blood pressure (increases, increase) the danger of serious heart problems for many people.

5. In the afternoon, I (tries, try) to be home by the time the school bus arrives.

6. There (has, have) been very little rainfall for the last two years; as a result, the drought has become more severe.

7. You don't (want, wants) to delay repairs any longer than necessary.

8. (Does, Do) anybody understand the new procedures well enough to train the temporary help?

9. As the doctor indicated, you must (takes, take) all of the prescribed medicine.

10. The new fast-food restaurant (brings, bring) customers to the old mall.

11. Many truck drivers (expects, expect) that the highway patrol will strictly enforce the sixty-five mile-per-hour speed limit.

12. Private companies increasingly (dumps, dump) toxic wastes in sites that are a hazard to community residents.

13. The citizens' watchdog group (is, are) lobbying for a reduction in health insurance rates.

14. Regardless of the reason for the attack, I (plans, plan) to press charges against the owner of the dog.

15. Parents of children with disabilities often (becomes, become) frustrated at many school systems' refusal to accommodate their children's special needs.

16. Jimmy Stewart (is, are) publishing his first book of poems at the age of 81.

17. Most people (avoid, avoids) going to the dentist because fees are so high.

18. Americans (eat, eats) 12 pounds of carrots, 118 pounds of potatoes, and 25 pounds of lettuce per person yearly.

19. If treated and removed in the earliest stages, most skin cancers (is, are) completely curable.

20. From August to October in the Midwest, over 250,000 tons of ragweed pollen (float, floats) through the air to cause us allergy problems.

≡≡≡Subject/Verb Agreement II

Review: 1. When two subjects are joined with a correlative conjunction (<u>either</u>, <u>or</u>; <u>neither</u>, <u>nor</u>; <u>whether</u>, <u>or</u>; <u>not only</u>, <u>but also</u>; <u>both</u>, <u>and</u>), the verb agrees in number with the subject closest to it.

Example: Neither my children nor their dog is out in the yard.

2. Some words are always singular (<u>anyone</u>, <u>everybody</u>) even though they refer to more than one. Review these words on page 109 of *Steck-Vaughn GED Writing Skills* book or other appropriate material.

Example: Everybody on my bowling team is here tonight.

Directions: Circle the correct word to complete each sentence.
Example: Not only the students but also the teacher (ⓘs, are) at lunch.

1. All of the migrant workers (anticipates, anticipate) the end of the harvest season.

2. Each of the packages (was, were) examined through the X-ray machine before being loaded on the plane.

3. Neither the lawyer nor her clients (believe, believes) the company's offer is satisfactory.

4. Both Mr. Rains and Mr. Sherrod (agrees, agree) that the important issue is how to protect the child from further abuse.

5. The secret tapes that contain the disputed conversation (was, were) accidentally misplaced.

6. Either the electrical wires or the light switch (was, were) installed improperly.

7. Few of the remaining parts (has, have) been examined for faults and, therefore, (needs, need) to be inspected before shipping to the assembly site.

8. Most of the employees (has, have) agreed to support the new union contract.

9. Everything, except for the programs, (has/have) been arranged for the graduation ceremony.

10. Several of the packages delivered yesterday (was/were) returned because they (was/were) not complete orders.

11. Whether the witness's statements or the evidence (was/were) falsified has yet to be determined.

12. Everybody at the meeting (expect, expects) the vote to be close.

13. Nothing, not even TV coverage of the droughts in Africa and the American Midwest, (has/have) resulted in reduced water usage by homeowners.

14. Neither the president of the company nor her advisors (want/wants) to take the risk of developing an unsafe product.

15. Not only butter but also many other dairy products (contains, contain) high levels of fat that can increase cholesterol levels.

16. Nobody, not even the parents who suggested the activities, (has, have) offered to supervise an event at the school carnival.

17. Both conscientious work and flexible skills (is, are) needed by a productive employee.

18. Not only Saudi Arabia but also several other countries in the Middle East (encourages, encourage) greater energy consumption by Americans.

19. Either Mrs. Payton or two other members of the club (is, are) responsible for the annual spring fund-raising event.

20. Any of the candidates who wish to attend the opening of the new senior citizens' center (needs, need) to notify the mayor's office by Tuesday.

21. Mrs. Jefferson informed the secretaries that neither the administrative assistant nor the vice-president (has, have) access to the confidential computer security codes.

22. None of the countries who signed the trade agreement (want, wants) to levy tariffs on imports.

Subject/Verb Agreement III

Directions: Determine if the verb used in each of the following sentences is correct. If so, write C in the blank. If the verb is not correct, write the correct form of the verb.

Example: When does the new employees start? _____ *do* _____

_____ 1. The construction of the new office buildings were delayed due to the unfavorable weather conditions this past spring.

_____ 2. This month there are several items that must be completed before we begin any new projects.

_____ 3. Where was the security officers during the robbery?

_____ 4. There was excitement in the office when the supervisor announced the availability of child care services.

_____ 5. The popularity of some insurance packages usually relate to their low monthly cost.

_____ 6. The habits one acquires as a child is often hard to break as an adult.

_____ 7. What is the evidence of his irresponsible actions?

_____ 8. Do the new videocassette recorder have a remote control unit?

_____ 9. The bus driver, in addition to her other responsibilities, check on the unattended children during the trip.

_____ 10. The recent bills from the phone company shows a new surcharge on local calls.

_____ 11. Portia Allen, one of the curators of the African American Museum of Art, have purchased some sculptures done in the South before the Civil War.

_____ 12. The famous athlete, appearing at several community events, is calling for a drug-free city.

_____ 13. Local officials caught in the middle of the situation says they do not receive enough state funding to continue the operation of the drug rehabilitation program.

_____ 14. There was three people in line ahead of me at the bank.

_____ 15. Who was the firefighters that rescued the family from the burning apartment?

≡≡≡Irregular Verbs I

Review: The past participle form of a verb needs a helping verb. If a helping verb is not present, use the simple past tense form.
>   **Example:** The phone <u>has</u> rung six times.

Directions: Write the correct form of the irregular verb (shown in parentheses) in the blank to complete each sentence.

Example: The phone _____*rang*_____ a lot today. (ring)

1. Because his car wouldn't start, Edwin was

   _____ for missing the crucial meeting. (forgive)

2. Have you _____ the letter of complaint about the defective blender to the company? (write)

3. What the action had _____ was anger the already frustrated homeowners. (do)

4. Mr. Harris, the man who had caused the

   accident, _____ the victim to the hospital. (take)

5. The Planning Commission has

   _____ permission to build a new shopping mall at the southeast end of town. (give)

6. Through an academic scholarship program,

   the university has _____ to recruit more minority students. (begin)

7. The proposed airport has

   _____ the property owners' chances of receiving fair bids on their homes since no one wants to live with the constant noise. (hurt)

8. After the press conference was over, the director of the health services department

   _____ about the free AIDS screening program. (speak)

9. After the telephone had

   _____ for five minutes without an answer, Mrs. Rivera decided to check on her elderly neighbor in person. (ring)

10. The sudden, violent hurricane

    _____ three mobile homes onto the highway before the residents could leave the area. (blow)

11. The mother had, for some time,

    _____ that the medical tests showed a promising recovery for her daughter who had leukemia, but she did not want to become overly optimistic. (knew)

12. At the funeral for Reverend Williams yesterday, the choir from Greater Love Baptist Church

    _____ several of his favorite hymns. (sing)

13. Because of the dangerous traffic, the

    children were _____ to cross the street unless accompanied by an adult. (forbid)

14. It was while he was boarding the bus to return to the army base that the soldier

    had _____ and broken his leg. (fall)

15. The damage to his lungs was

    _____ during the twenty years he had smoked menthol cigarettes. (do)

16. Almost everyone at the clinic yesterday

    _____ that the staff was helpful. (feel)

17. Has Mario _____ anything from the telephone company about his complaint? (hear)

≡≡≡Irregular Verbs II

Review: An irregular verb usually changes its spelling to form the past and past participle forms. Review the irregular verbs on pages 114–119 of *Steck-Vaughn GED Writing Skills* book or other appropriate materials.

Directions: Each of the following sentences has one error in verb usage. Circle the error and write the correct form of the verb in the blank following each sentence.

Example: I had (began) a two-week diet. ___*begun*___

1. While on her exercise program, Juanita jogged twice a week, attended an aerobic dance class once a week, and swum three times a week.

   _____

2. Houseplants often grow better when they are spray with a mixture of water and fertilizer.

   _____

3. Since Ivan had drove to the airport before, he knew that traffic might be heavy, so we left twenty minutes earlier than I had planned.

   _____

4. There was something wrong with the refrigerator since when I awoke on Tuesday morning everything, even the milk, had froze.

   _____

5. Make sure you knock loudly because the doorbell has been broke since last week.

   _____

6. As the ambulance attendant began to pack up his instruments, he told me it was fortunate we had called immediately since the child could have bleeded to death.

   _____

7. The police department has drawed up a plan to fight gang crime, but the plan hasn't yet been given to the chief for approval.

   _____

8. The car sank after it had went over the bridge into the river.

   _____

9. Because the robbery had occurred while she was actually in the house, she was shook by the fact that she could have been harmed if the thieves had known she was there.

   _____

10. I had forgot that many synthetic fabrics shrink when left in a hot dryer for an entire cycle.

    _____

11. When the recording artist sung her favorite song, my girlfriend pressed her hands against her lips and threw him a kiss.

    _____

12. Joshua had been surprised when Grandpa Myers had gave him the watch that had become a family heirloom.

    _____

13. On July 19, Norman Najimy speaked on a TV news show about inadequate funding for public education.

    _____

14. After you have took the clothes to the laundry, please go to the post office for stamps.

    _____

15. The restaurant notified all customers who had eat the seafood that some people had gotten sick.

    _____

16. After we had eaten dinner, I had washed the dishes.

    _____

≡≡Verb Tenses

Review: Tense is used to express past, present, or future time. All of the verbs in a sentence should have the same tense and reflect the appropriate time meaning of the sentence. Continuing tenses are used to show that action continues in the past (was sleeping), continues at the present time (is working), or will continue in the future (will be preparing).

Directions: Insert the correct verb form on the blank line in each sentence.

Example: I ___am working___ a ten-hour shift today. (work)

1. Automakers declared that during May new car sales _____ by over seven percent from the previous month. (decrease)

2. A survey in this month's *Parenting* magazine _____ that fathers don't do their fair share of childrearing and housework. (report)

3. Consumer groups say that if the U.S. Department of Agriculture doesn't hire more inspectors, the meat that we _____ in the future will have a higher chance of being contaminated. (purchase)

4. Pneumonia, the fifth leading cause of death in the U.S., _____ a major problem despite advances in treatment. (remain)

5. Last week, the federal government _____ a message to managers of professional sports teams to get tougher on drug violations by players. (send)

6. By next spring, most non-prescription sunglasses _____ labels telling how well they block harmful ultraviolet light. (has)

7. Many economists _____ that people, especially those who are young, are not saving enough money for their future retirement. (warn)

8. In the 1970's, many citizens _____ the environmental pollution concerns, and, as a result, some communities suffered a significant decrease in their air quality. (ignore)

9. The Kansas Highway Patrol reported yearly truck wrecks _____ 42.3% between 1981 and 1987. (increase)

10. Holland, Michigan, home of the annual Tulip Festival, _____ a competition each year for new tulip varieties. (sponsor)

11. When the politician _____ to take a blood alcohol test after the accident, he said it wasn't necessary and was a violation of his right to privacy. (refuse)

12. According to proposed legislation, the State Fire Marshall of North Dakota _____ that all fireworks during Fourth of July activities be banned. (request)

13. Currently, California's Wildlife and Parks Department _____ 50,000 trees to replace those burned during the forest fires of 1988. (plant)

14. The cost of prescription drugs _____ faster than other medical costs and faster than the rate of inflation. (rise)

Perfect Tense

Review: 1. The present perfect tense shows action that was completed in some indefinite time in the past or an action that began in the past and continues into the present. It is formed by using the helping verb <u>has</u> or <u>have</u> with the verb's past participle.
Example: She <u>has worked</u> here for several years.

2. The past perfect tense shows action that began and ended before another past action began. It is formed by using <u>had</u> with a past participle.
Example: You <u>had finished</u> working before I got here.

3. The future perfect tense shows future action that will begin and end before another future action begins. It is formed by using <u>shall have</u> or <u>will have</u> with a past participle.
Example: We <u>will have finished</u> working before dinner starts.

Directions: Complete each sentence by writing the correct perfect tense verb form in the blank.

Example: I had _____*seen*_____ that movie already. (see)

1. Because of the higher plane fares established last year, the number of passengers

   on trains _____ this year. (increase)

2. By the end of next year, the current popularity of neon-colored tennis shoes

   _____ .(decline)

3. Before leaving camp last year, the boys

   _____ how to tie several kinds of knots. (learn)

4. Before this last incident took place, I thought

   you _____ that if you broke the rules, you would automatically be punished. (understand)

5. Over 250,000 tourists _____ the theme park before the end of the summer season. (visit)

6. By the end of last week, management

   _____ all of the employees of the intended plant closing. (notify)

7. The airline _____ the plane two weeks prior to the accident. (inspect)

8. The disabled workers _____ that city buses be equipped with wheelchair lifts. (suggest)

9. The company's effort to clean up the

   contaminated wastes _____ before the court order was obtained. (begin)

10. After the divorce, Mary _____ a difficult time supporting the children until Frank began paying child support. (have)

11. For the last five years, Discount City

    _____ a child care service for its customers while they shop. (offer)

12. By the end of the day, the volunteers

    _____ flowers in each of the downtown planters to make the area more attractive. (plant)

13. Every week since they were married three years ago, Mr. and Mrs. Ling

    _____ at the Garden Spot Restaurant on Saturday night. (eat)

14. Next Wednesday the school board

    _____ whether to close the high school due to low enrollment. (decide)

15. In 2005, Michael Spence

    _____ for the company for fifteen years. (work)

16. Recently, the Food and Drug Administration

    _____ many drugs for sale over the counter. (approve)

Commonly Confused Verbs

Review: A few verbs need special attention since they are often used incorrectly.

Present	Past	Past Participle	(Meaning)
lie	lay	lain	(to recline or rest)
lay	laid	laid	(to place an object)
sit	set	set	(to place an object)
set	sat	sat	(to take a seat)
rise	rose	risen	(to go up or to get up)
raise	raised	raised	(to lift up)

Directions: Check the appropriate meaning needed in each of the following sentences. Then circle the correct verb form.

Example: He (lay, (laid)) his wallet on the dresser.

1. Because of increased property taxes, the landlord is (raising, rising) the rent next month.

2. The papers you are searching for are (lying, laying) on the desk in the office.

3. The office manager (sit, set) down the coffee on the conference table.

4. To make flaky pizza dough, let it (raise, rise) for at least an hour before placing it in the pans.

5. The dock worker asked the delivery man to (sit, set) boxes on the other end of the delivery platform.

6. The Queen Carpet Company had (laid, lain) the carpet in the house only two days before the Ortegas moved in.

7. Children learn responsibility by helping with minor tasks such as (sitting, setting) the table for dinner.

8. Mrs. Thomas had (laid, lain) in the hospital for two days before the police had been able to notify her children.

9. During our vacation in Atlantic City, I picked up over fifty shells I found (laying, lying) on the beach and brought them home.

10. In reference to the charges of mismanagement, the owner said, "You can believe we won't take this (sitting, setting) down."

11. When the patient had (rose, risen) the next morning, the pain had almost disappeared.

12. As we were driving east towards Pennsylvania, the sun was (raising, rising) over the horizon.

13. During the family reunion, my favorite cousin and I went outside and (lay, laid) under the trees where we had played for years.

14. According to some analysts, consumer prices have (raised, risen) in the past ten years because of higher manufacturing costs.

15. On the way home from the birthday party, our son (lay, laid) his presents on the back seat of the car.

16. I have (set, sat) on this bus and read many newspapers on my daily trips to work and home.

17. Smoke from the campfire (rose, raised) slowly in the still air.

18. By the time the holiday dinner was over, we had (set, sat) at the table for two hours.

19. Although we didn't know it at the time, the books we were searching for (laid, lay) on the floor of the closet.

20. By noon today, the divers will have (risen, raised) the treasure from the sunken ship.

21. Since Raymond was dizzy from the flu, he carefully (sat, set) his feet on the floor before he tried to stand up.

22. I need to (set, sit) down and rest for a few minutes.

Directions: Choose the best answer to each of the following items.

Items 1–12 refer to the following paragraph.

(1) About half of all fruits and vegetables contain some trace of the pesticides farmers uses to control harmful insects and fungi such as mold and mildew. (2) Some of these chemicals also preserve the nutritional value of food or improves it appearance. (3) The problem is that some of the pesticides may also caused cancer. (4) There are some precautions you can take if you're worried about the health of your family. (5) Washing all produce are important since water will remove some pesticides. (6) Even if it means losing some nutrients along with the pesticides, always peel fruits and vegetables. (7) Imported foods, which have twice the amount of pesticides as those grown in America, needs to be avoided. (8) The best-looking food is not always the best-tasting, and it may have been treated with a chemical "wax" that contained pesticide residue. (9) When using lettuce or cabbage, pull off the outer leaves since that is where pesticides are concentrated. (10) The best way to avoid pesticides, however, is to use fruits and vegetables that you have grewed yourself. (11) Then you can be sure that no pesticides was used. (12) However, if you're not a gardener you can buy only produce that will have been organically grown.

1. Sentence 1: **About half of all fruits and vegetables contain some trace of the pesticides farmers uses to control harmful insects and fungi such as mold and mildew.**

   What correction should be made to this sentence?

   (1) replace contain with contains
   (2) insert a comma after vegetables
   (3) replace uses with use
   (4) insert a comma after insects
   (5) no correction is necessary

2. Sentence 2: **Some of these chemicals also preserve the nutritional value of food or improves its appearance.**

   What correction should be made to this sentence?

   (1) replace preserve with preserves
   (2) insert a comma after value
   (3) insert a comma after food
   (4) replace improves with improve
   (5) no correction is necessary

3. Sentence 3: **The problem is that some of the pesticides may also caused cancer.**

   What correction should be made to this sentence?

   (1) change the spelling of problem to problam
   (2) replace is with was
   (3) insert a comma after some
   (4) replace caused with cause
   (5) no correction is necessary

4. Sentence 4: **There are some precautions you can take if you're worried about the health of your family.**

   Which of the following is the best way to write the underlined portion of this sentence? If you think the original is the best way, choose option (1).

   (1) you can take
   (2) you has taken
   (3) you may have taken
   (4) you had taken
   (5) you have had taken

5. Sentence 5: **Washing all produce are important since water will remove some pesticides.**

   What correction should be made to this sentence?

   (1) replace Washing with Wash
   (2) replace are with is
   (3) change the spelling of important to importent
   (4) insert a comma after important
   (5) no correction is necessary

6. Sentence 6: **Even if it means losing some nutrients along with the pesticides, always peel fruits and vegetables.**

   What correction should be made to this sentence?

   (1) replace losing with were losing
   (2) remove the comma after pesticides
   (3) replace peel with peels
   (4) change the spelling of vegetables to vegtables
   (5) no correction is necessary

7. Sentence 7: **Imported foods, which have twice the amount of pesticides as those grown in America, needs to be avoided.**

   What correction should be made to this sentence?

   (1) remove the comma after foods
   (2) replace have with has
   (3) insert comma after pesticides
   (4) replace needs with need
   (5) no correction is necessary

8. Sentence 8: **The best-looking food is not always the best-tasting, and it may have been treated with a chemical "wax" that contained pesticide residue.**

   Which of the following is the best way to write the underlined portion of this sentence? If you think the original is the best way, choose option (1).

   (1) that contained
   (2) that contains
   (3) that contain
   (4) that have contained
   (5) that was having contained

9. Sentence 9: **When using lettuce or cabbage, pull off the outer leaves since that is where pesticides are concentrated.**

   What correction should be made to this sentence?

   (1) remove the comma after cabbage
   (2) insert a comma after leaves
   (3) replace is with was
   (4) replace are with is
   (5) no correction is necessary

10. Sentence 10: **The best way to avoid pesticides, however, is to use fruits and vegetables that you have grewed yourself.**

    Which of the following is the best way to write the underlined portion of this sentence? If you think the original is the best way, choose the option (1).

    (1) that you have grewed
    (2) that you has grewed
    (3) that you may have been grown
    (4) that you have grown
    (5) that you were growing

11. Sentence 11: **Then you can be sure that no pesticides was used.**

    What correction should be made to this sentence?

    (1) replace can be with have been
    (2) insert a comma after sure
    (3) replace was with was being
    (4) replace was with were
    (5) no correction is necessary

12. Sentence 12: **However, if you're not a gardener, you can buy only produce that will have been organically grown.**

    What correction should be made to this sentence?

    (1) remove the comma after However
    (2) replace can buy with bought
    (3) insert a comma after produce
    (4) replace will have been with has been
    (5) no correction is necessary

≡Plural and Possessive Nouns

Review: 1. Plural nouns simply refer to more than one person, object, idea, or place.
   Example: I replaced the two front tires on my car.

   2. Possessive nouns use an apostrophe to show ownership. Singular possessive is spelled with 's. Plural possessive is spelled with s'.
   Example: My mother's car and my brothers' cars all need new tires.

   3. To decide whether a plural or a possessive noun form is needed, check the noun's meaning in the sentence. If the noun shows something else belongs to it, use the possessive form. For more help, see pages 66 and 87–88 in the *Steck-Vaughn GED Writing Skills* book or other appropriate material.

Directions: Circle the one incorrect plural or possessive noun in each of the following sentences. Write the correct form in the blank after each sentence.

Example: My (sisters) cat is gray. _____*sister's*_____

1. The mother's youngest child was the only one who had problem's with his teeth.

   _____

2. Students in China demonstrated to press the government to institute civil rights' such as freedom of speech.

   _____

3. The governments proposed funding cuts of veterans services has angered many Vietnam era veterans.

   _____

4. The man asked his children's permission to remarry to let them know that their opinions' were important to him.

   _____

5. Governor Lujan's plan to attract business's by providing them with tax incentives was applauded by the Better Business Association.

   _____

6. While following the deers trail, the three hunters recounted stories about memorable previous hunts.

   _____

7. The optometrist will test each eyes vision separately before she prescribes glasses or contact lenses.

   _____

8. A new state law protects public employees who expose co-workers' fraudulent practices from threats or retaliation by the agencys for whom the employees work.

   _____

9. After the searchers located the missing peoples, the Red Cross provided emergency medical attention and warm blankets.

   _____

10. The Transit Authority agreed yesterday to change four buses' routes in order to better serve the communitys surrounding Chicago.

    _____

11. Sunshine Food Market's prices are always lower than other grocery stores prices.

    _____

12. Harry accidentally dropped one of the bookcase's glass shelfs while he was unpacking the cartons.

    _____

13. The crashes impact completely destroyed the engine of the car, but fortunately the passengers weren't seriously injured.

    _____

14. The childrens health and safety must be the first concern of all day care centers.

    _____

≡ Personal Pronouns

Review: 1. A personal pronoun takes the place of a specific person, place, or thing. Some pronouns are used as subjects (<u>I</u>, <u>you</u>, <u>she</u>, <u>he</u>, <u>it</u>, <u>we</u>, <u>they</u>), and some pronouns are used as objects (<u>me</u>, <u>you</u>, <u>her</u>, <u>him</u>, <u>it</u>, <u>us</u>, <u>them</u>).
2. Some possessive pronouns (<u>my</u>, <u>your</u>, <u>his</u>, <u>her</u>, <u>its</u>, <u>our</u>, <u>your</u>, <u>their</u>) are used before nouns. Other possessive pronouns (<u>mine</u>, <u>yours</u>, <u>his</u>, <u>hers</u>, <u>ours</u>, <u>yours</u>, <u>theirs</u>) are used alone. Never use an apostrophe with a possessive pronoun.

Directions: Insert an appropriate pronoun in the blank in each of the following sentences. More than one pronoun form may be acceptable.

Example: I asked both of _____*them*_____ to join me.

1. Because he always complained about the insensitivity of the boss, _____ co-workers made _____ a form to check off his complaint of the day.

2. Children need to be exposed to different types of music, so I'm taking _____ with me to the concert.

3. Lillian and _____ were going to the hospital to visit his mother who had had surgery last Friday.

4. My husband and I were so surprised that the children gave an anniversary party for _____ .

5. After discussing the options, _____ decided to put our money together and buy a crib for the new parents.

6. Sarah said that the missing keys were _____ and that _____ appreciated everyone's help in locating them.

7. The child happily patted the puppy while it wagged _____ tail contentedly.

8. Our store is sorry to inconvenience _____ during the remodeling, and we appreciate _____ continued patronage.

9. Thank you for offering to help _____ repair the chair, but since I broke it, I think the responsibility to fix it is _____ .

10. We want to visit _____ at Easter since they came to _____ home at Christmas.

11. Please place _____ metal objects on the tray before you go through the security gate.

12. They indicated that the packages were _____, not the Bakers, as we had previously thought.

13. When the children came home from school, she asked _____ if they wanted a snack.

14. The O'Neill family and _____ decided to take a camping vacation together since our daughters are both Girl Scouts.

15. Both _____ and _____ will be considered for promotion to supervisor.

16. If _____ new pants don't fit, take _____ back to the store.

Pronoun Antecedents

Review: The word to which a pronoun refers is called an antecedent. A pronoun must agree with its antecedent in number (singular or plural), in gender (masculine, feminine, or neuter), and in person (first, second, or third).

Example: Mark and Amy have finished <u>their</u> lunch.

Directions: Circle the pronoun that is incorrectly used in each sentence. Complete the columns with the correct pronoun and antecedent for each.
The first one is completed as an example.

	Correct Pronoun	Antecedent
1. Mr. Peabody was having trouble completing (him) tax forms.	*his*	*Mr. Peabody*
2. After eating, the satisfied cat licked her paws.		
3. Together the Baileys and they agreed to share them expenses for the repairs.		
4. The old house with plenty of storage space and a large yard has their good points.		
5. Both Edward and Allan have had his difficulties with the law.		
6. Like the neighbor, Ms. Gutierrez is planting their garden early this year.		
7. Felicia couldn't recall which box did not have their top sealed.		
8. Either Jennifer or Maxine is providing their own food for lunch.		
9. You may forget the duffel bag if you leave them in the locker room during our aerobics class.		
10. Neither Jimmy nor Sam brought along them pictures of the wedding.		
11. The people of France celebrated the 200th anniversary of them independence with fireworks and parades.		
12. Mother Nature brought early spring rains, and its efforts produced thousands of colorful flowers.		
13. Americans sure like they popcorn; in one year they ate 24 million pounds of cheese-flavored popcorn.		
14. This computer program has her quirks, but is still easy to use.		
15. The parents were worried when them children were late coming home from school.		

≡Indefinite Pronoun Antecedents

Review: 1. Indefinite pronouns do not refer to particular persons or things.

Singular Pronouns			Plural Pronouns	
anybody	everyone	nothing	both	many
anyone	everything	one	few	several
each	neither	somebody		
either	nobody	someone		
everybody	no one			

2. A pronoun that refers to an indefinite pronoun antecedent must agree with that pronoun in gender, number, and person.
   Example: Neither of the cats got <u>its</u> dinner.

Directions: Circle the pronoun in parentheses that agrees with the antecedent.
Example: Several of the tomato plants lost (its, ⊙their⊙) leaves.

1. Each of the truck drivers received (his, their) mileage check and new load orders.

2. Every one of the electricians has (his, their) own tools and supplies.

3. We will not be able to accomplish our objectives if everyone won't do (his, their) fair share of the work.

4. Several of the women bought (herself, themselves) ceramic statues at the museum party.

5. Perhaps one of the international tourists accidentally left (his, their) camera at the airport.

6. Anyone who can provide proof of purchase will have (his, their) money refunded.

7. Neither of the sales representatives was granted (her, their) request for a transfer.

8. Both of the caseworkers were informed of (his, their) reassignment to the emergency investigation unit.

9. If everyone wanted to schedule (his, their) vacation in July, it would cause production problems.

10. Each of the samples arrived in (its, their) own package.

11. A few were informed that (he, they) would be laid off at the end of August.

12. Nobody, not even the kids who were involved, would tell (his, their) side of the story.

13. Either Ben or Zack will have to admit the truth about (his, their) involvement in the accident.

14. Because of the delay in processing, neither of the ladies received (her, their) order within six weeks as promised.

15. There has been a great deal of confusion about whether anyone can file (his, their) case in small claims court.

16. Many of the employees want (its, their) insurance claims to be filed by Personnel.

17. No one wants (his or her, their) taxes to increase, but most people want more services from government.

18. Everybody in the group of expectant mothers wanted to add to (her, their) knowledge about raising children.

19. If anybody in the Men's Garden Club wants to bring (his, their) spouse to the meeting, visitors are always welcome.

20. A few of the players on the softball team said that (he, they) could practice after work.

21. One of the nurses said that (she, they) could work a double shift.

22. My uncle always said, "Everything has (its, his) price."

23. If somebody knows a better procedure, (they, she) should tell the manufacturing supervisor.

24. No one wants to give up (his or her, their) place in line.

≡ Pronoun Errors

Review: Subject pronouns must be used in compound subjects. When used with nouns, pronouns are always placed last. A subject pronoun is also used when a pronoun in the predicate refers to the subject and follows a linking verb.
Example: The winner of the race was she.

Directions: Rewrite the following sentences, correcting any pronoun errors.
Example: Me and my friend went out to eat.

My friend and I went out to eat.

1. Terry, Jose, and him took their wives out to dinner together.

   _____

   _____

2. Tonight us and the Browns are going to see the just released movie.

   _____

   _____

3. The general did not know it was them who arrived at the military base.

   _____

   _____

4. The reporter asked if it was me who reported the fire.

   _____

   _____

5. While playing at the park, him and the children found a stray cat that they brought home.

   _____

   _____

6. After the wedding, Mr. and Mrs. Santucci and them stopped by the house before going to the reception.

   _____

   _____

7. Gina and me would like to take courses to improve our computer skills.

   _____

   _____

≣ Who/Whom

Review: 1. <u>Who</u> and <u>whoever</u> are used as subjects.
       Example: Who left the front door open?
    2. <u>Whom</u> and <u>whomever</u> are used as objects.
       Example: Whom did you invite to our party?

Directions: Circle the correct pronoun choice in each of the following sentences.
Example: To (who, (whom)) did you send invitations?

1. When you went to the company to complain about the poor service, to (who, whom) did you speak?

2. The parents (who, whom) were not included in the discussion were angry.

3. Bill asked him for (who, whom) he was working now.

4. You may choose (whoever, whomever) you wish to help you with this task.

5. The radio announcer could not contact Mrs. Battle, (who, whom) was the winner of their contest.

6. The environmentalists (who, whom) have spoken out against the nuclear power plant have scheduled a demonstration for Sunday.

7. To (who, whom) do you want this package to be sent?

8. Sandra, (who, whom) worked very hard, was given a bonus for her dedication.

9. She believed that (whoever, whomever) you are referring to did not know about the possible side effects of that drug.

10. The only suspect (who, whom) the police arrested was the one who had the weapon in his possession.

11. Only people (who, whom) have car insurance are permitted to drive in Florida.

12. Martin Luther King, Jr., (who, whom) was given a Nobel Peace Prize, believed in nonviolent means to achieve progress.

13. (Whoever, Whomever) left his wallet in the cafeteria can claim it in the Security Office.

14. The heart rate of a person (who, whom) wants to benefit from aerobic exercise should be between 18–28 beats every 10 seconds.

15. (Whoever, Whomever) said that didn't understand all of the facts regarding the transmission of AIDS.

16. Mr. Wright, (who, whom) I've known all of my life, has always demonstrated kindness and patience towards other people.

17. The leader (who, whom) demonstrates the characteristics of honesty and perseverance is often the one (who, whom) gets results.

18. The woman (who, whom) had an allergic reaction to the medicine is now resting comfortably.

19. The person (who, whom) I can recommend for the job is Clarence Arnold.

20. The men and women (who, whom) demonstrated for equal rights in the 1970's will be remembered for their courage.

21. Nancy Reagan, (who, whom) was First Lady while Ronald Reagan was President, has since written a book of her memoirs.

22. Please take this computer printout to (whoever, whomever) needs the data.

23. The police officer (who, whom) stopped my car asked me to show proof that I have insurance.

24. Most students (who, whom) have used interactive video instruction like the immediate feedback they receive.

25. The weather forecaster (who, whom) I like is leaving the local TV station and moving to another city.

26. The candidate opened his campaign speech by saying, "(Who, Whom) can we trust if we can't trust our elected officials?"

≡ Homonyms

Review: 1. Some pronouns are confused with words that sound like them.
   It's: a contraction of the pronoun it and the verb is
   Its: a possessive pronoun showing ownership
2. They're: a contraction of the pronoun they and the verb are
   There: an adverb that shows direction
   Their: a possessive pronoun that shows ownership
3. Who's: a contraction of the pronoun who and the verb is
   Whose: a pronoun showing possession
4. You're: a contraction of the pronoun you and the verb are
   Your: a possessive pronoun

Directions: Insert the correct word from the list above in the blank in each of the following sentences.

Example: You're going to need _____*your*_____ umbrella today.

1. The store that sells only cookies will open _____ third site next week in the mall.

2. The person _____ responsible has not yet been identified.

3. _____ very fortunate that she was offered a scholarship; she wouldn't have been able to attend otherwise.

4. Due to their past involvement, _____ being asked to help the new volunteers learn their responsibilities.

5. The packing crates we need are over _____ by the wall.

6. The child _____ parents encourage good study habits usually does well in school.

7. Please bring _____ suggestions regarding safety to the next meeting.

8. The McDonald family took _____ dog with them when they went to visit Mrs. McDonald's mother in Florida.

9. The City Council changed _____ position on gun control after the shooting incident.

10. _____ being asked to bring a dish for your company picnic.

11. While good nutrition is important, _____ also necessary to get an adequate amount of exercise.

12. To register for any job listed on the board, you must have _____ social security card with you.

13. The actor _____ most popular at any given time usually has a special, innocent look about him or her.

14. The couple asked _____ real estate agent to recommend the best way to finance a house within their budget.

15. Because _____ so organized, they can get a lot accomplished each day.

16. When the doctor arrived at the emergency room, her patient had already been waiting _____ for over an hour.

17. Can you tell _____ handwriting this is?

18. The builders don't know yet when _____ going to begin construction.

≡ Adjectives

Review: 1. To compare two people, places, or things, use the comparative degree (words usually ending in -er or using more).
Example: Can you work faster or more productively?

2. To compare more than two people, places, or things, use the superlative degree (words usually ending in -est or using most). Never use more or most with adjectives ending in -er or -est.
Example: You are the most productive employee we have.

Directions: Each of the following sentences contains an error in adjective usage. Circle the error and correct it on the line below.
Example: Can you get to work (more earlier)?

earlier

1. Between Derrick and Paul, Derrick has the best chance of being promoted.

   _____

2. Of all the people I know, Louise is the more patient.

   _____

3. We're going to buy the used car because it's least expensive than the new car we wanted but couldn't afford.

   _____

4. At the restaurant, we saw the most biggest lobster we've ever seen.

   _____

5. It is difficulter than I thought it would be to put up patterned wall paper.

   _____

6. The fender of the car was more smoother after the repair shop finished it.

   _____

7. Mrs. Carter, who has seen many exotic plants, remarked that this was the more unusual one.

   _____

8. Because of the deadline, everyone had to work more faster.

   _____

9. Of the two neighbors who often enjoyed the warm summer evenings, the Reeds' patio was always neatest.

   _____

10. My husband feels comfortable here than at my mother's house, so we appreciate your letting us stay for the night.

    _____

11. Because snow drifts on this road, it is the dangerousest road in the county.

    _____

12. He said he felt most rested today than he did yesterday.

    _____

13. That area of the city seems to be more quiet than any other.

    _____

14. I was attracted to him because I thought he was the funnier man I had ever met.

    _____

15. It was hard to tell who was the angriest, Mr. Chappell or Mr. Warner.

    _____

16. Of the two instructors, I really preferred the oldest one.

    _____

Directions: Choose the best answer for each of the following items.

Items 1–11 refer to the following paragraph.

(1) A symbol of America's abundance are the supermarket, which has been part of the national scene since the first one opened in the 1930's. (2) At many stores, the variety of produce, meat, dairy, and paper products is overwhelming. (3) In the produce section, a customer can discover over sixty types of fruit. (4) In addition to the typical fruits like peaches strawberries, and blueberries, items like kiwi, persimmons, mangoes, and tamarillos are available. (5) Some supermarkets provide nontraditional services as well; for example babysitting is being provided by some stores. (6) Other supermarkets are opening dry cleaning services, so customers can drop off and pick up their clothes when they does their weekly shopping. (7) Still other supermarkets had begun to offer space to local artists who display and sell their handiwork in the store. (8) Each of these features, say the managers, attracts customers whom otherwise would go elsewhere. (9) Huge supermarkets, called superstores, not only offers food items but also sell clothes, appliances, car repair items, household goods, and furniture under one roof. (10) Critics say these superstores are simply too large for most people to feel more comfortable shopping in them. (11) By examining supermarkets and superstores, it is easy to see the variety, service, and convenience to which most Americans has access.

1. Sentence 1: **A symbol of America's abundance are the supermarket, which has been part of the national scene since the first one opened in the 1930's.**

   What correction should be made to this sentence?

   (1) replace America's with Americas
   (2) replace are with is
   (3) replace has with have
   (4) insert a comma after scene
   (5) no correction is necessary

2. Sentence 2: **At many stores, the variety of produce, meat, dairy, and paper products is overwhelming.**

   (1) remove the comma after stores
   (2) change the spelling of variety to vareity
   (3) insert a comma after products
   (4) replace is with are
   (5) no correction is necessary

3. Sentence 3: **In the produce section, a customer can discover over sixty types of fruit.**

   What correction should be made to this sentence?

   (1) remove the comma after section
   (2) replace can with did
   (3) change the spelling of discover to discuver
   (4) insert a comma after sixty
   (5) no correction is necessary

4. Sentence 4: **In addition to the typical fruits like peaches strawberries, and blueberries, items like kiwi, persimmons, mangoes, and tamarillos are available.**

   What correction should be made to this sentence?

   (1) insert a comma after addition
   (2) change the spelling of familiar to familure
   (3) insert a comma after peaches
   (4) remove the comma after blueberries
   (5) no correction is necessary

5. Sentence 5: **Some supermarkets provide nontraditional services as well; for example babysitting is being provided by some stores.**

   Which of the following is the best way to write the underlined portion of this sentence? If you think the original is the best way, choose option (1).

   (1) as well; for example
   (2) as well, for example
   (3) as well, for example,
   (4) as well; for example,
   (5) as well for example

6. Sentence 6: **Other supermarkets are opening dry cleaning services, so customers can drop off and pick up their clothes when they does their weekly shopping.**

   What correction should be made to this sentence?

   (1) remove the comma after services
   (2) insert a comma after off
   (3) replace does with do
   (4) replace their with they're
   (5) no correction is necessary

7. Sentence 7: **Still other supermarkets had begun to offer space to local artists who display and sell their handiwork in the store.**

   Which of the following is the best way to write the underlined portion of this sentence? If you think the original is the best way, choose option (1).

   (1) had begun to offer
   (2) are beginning to offer
   (3) is beginning to offer
   (4) have began to offer
   (5) began to offer

8. Sentence 8: **Each of these features, say the managers, attracts customers whom otherwise would go elsewhere.**

   What corrections should be made to this sentence?

   (1) remove the comma after features
   (2) replace say with says
   (3) replace attracts with attract
   (4) replace whom with who
   (5) no correction is necessary

9. Sentence 9: **Huge supermarkets, called superstores, not only offers food items but also sell clothes, appliances, car repair items, household goods, and furniture under one roof.**

   Which of the following is the best way to write the underlined portion of this sentence? If you think the original is the best way, choose option (1).

   (1) not only offers food
   (2) not only offer food
   (3) not only has food to offer
   (4) had offered not only
   (5) has been offering not only

10. Sentence 10: **Critics say these superstores are simply too large for most people to feel more comfortable shopping in them.**

    What correction should be made to this sentence?

    (1) replace say with says
    (2) replace are with is
    (3) insert a comma after people
    (4) remove more
    (5) no correction is necessary

11. Sentence 11: **By examining supermarkets and superstores, it is easy to see the variety, service, and convenience to which most Americans has access.**

    What correction should be made to this sentence?

    (1) remove the comma after superstores
    (2) replace easy with easier
    (3) change the spelling of convenience to conveneince
    (4) replace has with have
    (5) no correction is necessary

Items 12–23 refer to the following paragraph.

(1) If your parents are elderly, you may worry at times about where they'll live when they can no longer take care of themselves. (2) Elderly parents can't always live with they're adult children because of the children's limited space or other responsibilities. (3) There are now many more living options for elderly people than there was. (4) In a shared housing arrangement, two or more older people, usually unrelated, shares a house or apartment. (5) This option provides companionship and some security for your parents', since they may live independently but not be alone in case of emergencies. (6) Another option is a retirement community where services keeps pace with the changing needs of the residents. (7) A retirement community provides independence for your parents, but it also provides housekeeping assistance or home health care if necessary. (8) An advantage of retirement communities is their organized activities and programs that keep them active. (9) Their is always something to do. (10) If a resident aren't able to cook anymore, meals can be eaten at a cafeteria or delivered to the person's apartment. (11) Either of these options are suitable for elderly people who don't have major health problems. (12) Together with your parents, pick an option that suits your parents' lifestyle, temperment, and financial situation. (13) You and them can make the right choice together.

12. Sentence 2: **Elderly parents can't always live with they're adult children because of the children's limited space or other responsibilities.**

What correction should be made to this sentence?

(1) replace they're with their
(2) replace children's with childrens
(3) insert a comma after space
(4) change the spelling of responsibilities to responsibilitys
(5) no correction is necessary

13. Sentence 3: **There are now many more living options for elderly people <u>than there was.</u>**

Which of the following is the best way to write the underlined portion of this sentence? If you think the original is the best way, choose option (1).

(1) than there was
(2) than there had been
(3) but then there was
(4) then was there
(5) than could have been

14. Sentence 4: **In a shared housing arrangement, two or more older people, usually unrelated, shares a house or apartment.**

What correction should be made to this sentence?

(1) change the spelling of arrangement to arrangment
(2) remove the comma after arrangement
(3) change the spelling of usually to usaully
(4) remove the comma after unrelated
(5) replace shares with share

15. Sentence 5: **This option provides companionship and some security for your parents', since they may live independently but not be alone in case of emergencies.**

What correction should be made to this sentence?

(1) replace provides with provide
(2) replace parents' with parents
(3) remove the comma after parents'
(4) change the spelling of independently to independantly
(5) no correction is necessary

16. Sentence 6: **Another option is a retirement community where services keeps pace with the changing needs of the residents.**

    What correction should be made to this sentence?

    (1) replace is with are
    (2) insert a comma after retirement
    (3) replace keeps with keep
    (4) insert a comma after needs
    (5) no correction is necessary

17. Sentence 7: **A retirement community provides independence for your parents, but it also provides housekeeping assistance or home health care if necessary.**

    What correction should be made to this sentence?

    (1) replace community with communitys
    (2) replace provides with provide
    (3) replace it with them
    (4) change the spelling of assistance to assistence
    (5) no correction is necessary

18. Sentence 8: **An advantage of retirement communities is their organized activities and programs that keep them active.**

    What correction should be made to this sentence?

    (1) change the spelling of advantage to advantege
    (2) replace is with are
    (3) replace their with they're
    (4) replace them with elderly people
    (5) no correction is necessary

19. Sentence 9: **Their is always something to do.**

    What correction should be made to this sentence?

    (1) change the spelling of Their to Thier
    (2) replace Their with There
    (3) replace is with are
    (4) change the spelling of always to allways
    (5) no correction is necessary

20. Sentence 10: **If a resident aren't able to cook anymore, meals can be eaten at a cafeteria or delivered to the person's apartment.**

    Which of the following is the best way to write the underlined portion of this sentence? If you think the original is the best way, choose option (1).

    (1) aren't able to cook
    (2) isn't able to cook
    (3) hasn't been able to cook
    (4) having not been able to cook
    (5) had not been able to cook

21. Sentence 11: **Either of these options are suitable for elderly people who don't have major health problems.**

    What correction should be made to this sentence?

    (1) replace are with is
    (2) insert a comma after people
    (3) replace who with whom
    (4) replace don't with doesn't
    (5) no correction is necessary

22. Sentence 12: **Together with your parents, pick an option that suits your parents' lifestyle, temperment, and financial situation.**

    What correction should be made to this sentence?

    (1) remove the comma after parents
    (2) insert a semicolon after option
    (3) replace parents' with parent's
    (4) change the spelling of temperment to temperament
    (5) no correction is necessary

23. Sentence 13: **You and them can make the right choice together.**

    What correction should be made to this sentence?

    (1) replace them with they
    (2) replace right with rite
    (3) change the spelling of together to togeter
    (4) remove together
    (5) no correction is necessary

Unit 3 Sentence Structure

Sentence Fragments

Review: A sentence must have a subject and a predicate and must express a complete thought.
    Example: The Supreme Court members announced a ruling on the case about flag burning.

Directions: Identify each of the following groups of words by writing an <u>F</u> if the group of words is a fragment, or by writing an <u>S</u> if it is a sentence. Then, on another sheet of paper, rewrite the fragments as complete sentences.

Example: __*S*__ This sentence contains a subject and a verb.

_____ 1. A class of adults learning about how to make their own car repairs.

_____ 2. Police crackdowns could raise adult drug arrests by about 80 percent.

_____ 3. The laborers' union council to decide what sites to picket.

_____ 4. Charged with drunken driving after falling asleep at a traffic light.

_____ 5. Mr. Contreras, the only resident who is against the plan.

_____ 6. Plans to buy the deluxe vacuum cleaner since it is on sale.

_____ 7. The State Representative challenged the state-operated lottery, but his challenge was voted down.

_____ 8. A survey of twenty-two cities that are considering new property taxes.

_____ 9. To combat child abuse, the agency has requested an additional thirty social workers.

_____ 10. To repair over half of the state's crumbling bridges.

_____ 11. After deciding on going to the lake and buying the necessary fishing permits.

_____ 12. The low-income housing project which will be located near Huntley Park.

_____ 13. A prison construction project could employ over one hundred community residents.

_____ 14. Over two thousand people attended the annual Malcolm X Day in honor of the slain civil rights leader's birthday.

_____ 15. Educators planning to boycott the reduction of funds for the community college library's computer system.

_____ 16. The brown shrimp harvest is expected to be the biggest in three years.

_____ 17. Most of the drug-related deaths reported in 1995.

_____ 18. On the way to the local discount store, seeing a video store's offer of three movies for $5.00.

_____ 19. To discuss the role of women in history, a three-day conference is planned.

_____ 20. The school committee member, arguing that "children have the right to know how to protect themselves."

_____ 21. Soccer is a popular sport all over the world.

_____ 22. When the polls have closed and all the votes have finally been counted.

See Also Steck-Vaughn GED Writing Skills   Unit 3
Steck-Vaughn Complete GED Preparation   Unit 1, Sentence Structure

Run-On Sentences

Review: Run-on sentences are two or more sentences strung together in one very long sentence. The run-on expresses two or more complete thoughts and confuses readers. Run-on sentences can usually be corrected by separating the ideas into two or more sentences. Run-ons can also be corrected by using appropriate conjunctions and punctuation.

Example: Jake got a speeding ticket; he is taking a defensive driving course.

Jake got a speeding ticket. He will take a defensive driving course.

Jake got a speeding ticket, so he is taking a defensive driving course.

Since Jake got a speeding ticket, he will take a defensive driving course.

Directions: Rewrite one of the two paragraphs below, correcting any run-on sentences. Add words as necessary to form complete sentences.

Paragraph 1:

People who have been divorced know that the breakup of a marriage can leave deep scars on their children who often think they are at fault for the divorce and blame themselves for being "bad" children. Children are also afraid that they will become latchkey kids, sometimes they fear that they will become homeless or have to live in a shelter, or they may have fantasies about the absent parent returning, or become victims of custody battles and have to choose between their mother and father.

Paragraph 2:

The credit card industry is less than forty years old and some credit cards have offered real convenience, those accepting credit cards include hospitals for open-heart surgery and the federal government for income taxes. Credit cards have made debt the American way of life so instead of saving for a washer and dryer people merely charge them but do not realize that it may cost them more to charge than to pay cash. As a result of easy access to credit, many American families are over their heads in debt.

_____

_____

_____

_____

_____

_____

_____

_____

_____

_____

_____

_____

≣Sentence Combining I

Review: Two related sentences are often joined with a linking word (conjunction) to form one compound sentence. The conjunction must properly reflect the meaning of the sentence. Some common linking words include: <u>and</u>, <u>nor</u>, <u>but</u>, <u>otherwise</u>, <u>consequently</u>, <u>or</u>, <u>however</u>, <u>for example</u>, <u>in addition</u>, and <u>meanwhile</u>. Refer to page 7 to review punctuation.

Example: I read the list of apartments for rent; however, none accepts pets.

Directions: Insert an appropriate linking word from the list above in the blank in each of the sentences below. Add correction punctuation if needed.

Example: I may look for an apartment today, _____ _or_ _____ I may wait until tomorrow.

1. Computers perform many repetitive tasks _____ they cannot replace people's ability to think.

2. The woman had little hope for recovery _____ her husband believed she could fight the disease.

3. Do you want to spend the evening at home watching TV _____ would you rather go bowling?

4. The traffic was heavier than usual _____ we were late for our appointment.

5. You need to inspect each part carefully _____ you may miss some of the defective ones.

6. Exercise helps to strengthen your heart _____ it also helps to control your weight.

7. The government sometimes wastes money _____ it paid $6.00 apiece for door hinges which cost about seventy-five cents at a hardware store.

8. Plants are not very expensive gifts _____ they are readily available almost everywhere.

9. I like onions _____ I can't eat them.

10. In Illinois, citizens were encouraged to spend more money _____ in Texas, citizens were urged to put more of their money in savings accounts.

11. You cannot smoke in that part of the building _____ can you have food or drink there.

12. I really like living on the West Coast _____ I miss the change of seasons in the Midwest.

13. You have completed the probationary period successfully _____ you are eligible for union membership.

14. The homeowners obviously didn't know about the flood conditions _____ they would have begun making preparations for it sooner.

15. Many people aren't interested in local politics _____ only one-sixth of the city residents voted in the last election.

16. This brand of toilet tissue is more expensive _____ it is softer and has more sheets per roll.

17. There are many lifestyle changes people can make to achieve better health _____ two important ones are eating a balanced diet and getting more exercise.

≡ Sentence Combining II

Review: There are several ways to combine sentences. Sometimes one sentence can be changed into a phrase or a dependent clause. Other times, sentences can be joined with the appropriate coordinate conjunction (<u>and</u>, <u>but</u>, <u>or</u>, <u>nor</u>, <u>for</u>, <u>yet</u>). When combining sentences, check the new sentence for correct punctuation.

   Examples: Some people prefer city living, yet others prefer the country.
   While some people prefer the city, others prefer the country.

Directions: For each group of sentences below, combine them and write a new sentence on another sheet of paper. Check your punctuation.

Example: Joyce received on-the-job-training with computers. Now she's able to sell computers and

train others. *Joyce received on-the-job training*

with computers, and now she's able to sell computers and

train others.

1. Advanced Business System's training program was very costly. Their record of job placement was excellent.

2. The police officer is very efficient. She often gets tired of the paperwork.

3. He bought a new set of carpet mats for the car. They were on sale last week.

4. Most brands of lunch meat contain artificial preservatives. Artificial preservatives are used to retard spoilage.

5. We can leave for the restaurant soon. I need to make these phone calls first.

6. I will finish washing the windows. Could you please mow the lawn?

7. Some companies use drug testing. It is a standard part of their pre-employment process.

8. Grocery stores in the inner city and the suburbs are often run by the same company. There are often differences in prices for the same product.

9. "Happy Days Are Here Again" was a popular song. It was one of the most well-known songs of the 1930's.

10. The package was mailed on Wednesday by Mrs. Sinata. It was addressed to her grandchild.

11. The report caused controversy within the agency. It was recently filed by the Internal Investigation Unit.

12. The list showed that fees vary widely. Lawyers charged from $225 to $2,500 for an uncontested divorce.

13. The Disney-MGM Studios Theme Park is near Orlando, Florida. It cost $500 million to build.

14. General Motors' Corvette ZR1 has a top speed of 180 m.p.h. This car can go from 0 to 60 m.p.h. in 4.2 seconds.

15. Scientists R. Stanley Pons and Martin Fleischmann claimed they found a simpler way to generate fusion. Many other scientists said that their work was flawed.

16. I had a car accident when I was sixteen. I had nightmares for ten years afterward.

17. Child safety seats have become important devices. They reduce injury to children in car accidents.

18. It will stop raining soon. We can go for a walk or to the park.

19. A VCR allows viewers to tape TV shows. The shows can be watched at a more convenient time.

≡ Parallel Structure

Review: Parallel sentence structure involves making sure that related words or phrases within a sentence are in similar form. When a series of verbs, nouns, adjectives, adverbs, or phrases is joined with a linking word, make all the items parallel in form.

Examples: (Not Parallel) The leader of the group is shrewd, tough, and has power.
(Parallel): The leader of the group is shrewd, tough, and powerful.

Directions: Circle the part of each sentence below that is not parallel. Then rewrite the sentence in correct form on another sheet of paper.

Example: The car is sleek, sturdy, (and has a lot of room).

The car is sleek, sturdy, and roomy.

1. The residents volunteered to board up abandoned buildings, wash graffiti off the walls, and are patrolling the park.

2. The employees were asked to stock the shelves, take inventory, and were sweeping the floor.

3. Beginning the preparations now will be better than to postpone them.

4. To prevent crime, both police protection and involving the community are necessary.

5. Mr. Cutter thinks travel is exciting because it allows him an opportunity to meet new people and for seeing different places.

6. The hospital staff asked the patient for his name, his address, and what his phone number was.

7. People tend to exercise more regularly if they take part in more than one activity; for example, a person could alternate bicycling, walking, and to swim occasionally.

8. It's quiet now because Josh is sleeping. Trina is playing outside, and Brian decided to read a book.

9. On the weekends we enjoy going out to eat, the shopping malls, and driving in the country.

10. Many fast food restaurants' milkshakes are not made with milk but with fillers, flavorings, and many have added chemicals.

11. When examining a house, always check for water marks on the walls, how much pressure the water faucets have, and sediment in the pipes.

12. A small family business has a better chance of being profitable if its product is unique, uses common ingredients, and the prices are fairly low cost.

13. To live well requires a belief in one's self, an attitude of fairness, and having a desire to help others.

14. Using fertilizer, watering regularly, and making sure to weed every week can improve the harvest from your garden.

15. The Bill of Rights guarantees our freedom of speech, our right to assemble peacefully, and we have the right to bear arms.

16. Neither exercising nor to eat less food is the best way to lose weight; the best way is to combine the two.

17. Good books, watching movies, and softball are three of my favorite hobbies.

18. At noon I'll deposit my paycheck, put gas in the car, and we need some bread.

19. To paint pictures and playing music are two ways for individuals to express their creativity.

20. The special dinner at China Palace comes with egg rolls, fried rice, and you get wonton soup.

≣≣Subordination I

Review: Subordination is joining ideas of lesser importance to a main idea. To use subordination correctly, first identify the main idea and the subordinate idea in a sentence. Then use an appropriate subordinating word to link the ideas. The resulting sentence should be clear and logical.

Examples of subordinating words and their purposes are below:

Cause and Effect		**Comparison**	
because	in order to	as much as	as if
even if	in order that	as well as	just as
unless	so that	considering that	

Contrasts		**Time Related**	
although	unlike	as	since
though	whereas	after	until
unless	while	as soon as	before
		whenever	while

Directions: On another sheet of paper, combine the sentences in each group, using a subordinating word that expresses the logical connection.

Example: I have to go to the store. I ran out of coffee.

I have to go to the store because I ran out

of coffee.

1. Johnson has to leave early. He has to pick up his son from the day care center.

2. The hurricane had destroyed the mobile home park. The federal government provided emergency assistance.

3. Newspapers can give specific details of a story. Television news usually only reports the general outline.

4. Tooth decay has decreased significantly. This is probably because toothpastes now contain fluoride.

5. The quality of future life depends on us. The Environmental Protection Agency wants to act now to protect the environment.

6. We could save enough money for the down payment. We would still need to have money for moving costs and initial repairs.

7. I will take Mother to visit her friends. I will stop at the cleaners and drop off the clothes.

8. The new findings show that dairy products contain fat. They also contain calcium and vitamins.

9. I would like to go with you. I have to care for my sister's children since she's in the hospital.

10. The problem of drug use needs to be addressed. Many of our children will become victims.

11. I don't get home from work until after 6:00. I miss seeing the 5:30 TV news shows every day.

12. My dental hygienist is gentle and does not cause me discomfort when she cleans my teeth. I plan to continue getting my teeth cleaned every six months.

13. I will save money from my paycheck this month. I will be able to buy a new CD player.

14. The band has been playing much better recently. They have been practicing a lot and learning new material.

≋Subordination II

Directions: Review the subordinating words on page 47. Then circle the letter before the sentence in each pair which uses a subordinating word that best conveys the meaning of the sentence.

Example: (a.) When I have time, I'll wash the car.
   b.   Unlike I have time, I'll wash the car.

1. a. Before the account is paid in full, the electricity will be turned back on.
   b. As soon as the account is paid in full, the electricity will be turned back on.

2. a. I am sure she will get the promotion, considering how well she has done her job in the past.
   b. I am sure she will get the promotion, though she has done her job well in the past.

3. a. Because the tavern was closing for the night, the customers were asked to leave.
   b. The tavern was closing for the night since the customers were asked to leave.

4. a. Even though the medication relieves the pain, it causes her to be nauseated.
   b. Unless it causes her to be nauseated, the medication relieves the pain.

5. a. Because the manager denied being at the store, a clerk saw him leave through the back door.
   b. Although a clerk saw him leave through the back door, the manager denied being at the store.

6. a. Some women said that even if child care were available, they would register for classes.
   b. Some women said that as soon as child care was available, they would register for classes.

7. a. Because AIDS is such a devastating disease, many people are becoming more cautious.
   b. Even if AIDS is such a devastating disease, many people are becoming more cautious.

8. a. Since you were out of the office, you received many telephone calls.
   b. While you were out of the office, you received many telephone calls.

9. a. Until the lottery jackpot goes over 20 million dollars, more people tend to buy tickets.
   b. Whenever the lottery jackpot goes over 20 million dollars, more people tend to buy tickets.

10. a. After providing convenience to their customers, many banks have installed automated cash machines.
    b. In order to provide convenience for their customers, many banks have installed automated cash machines.

11. a. When children are given a choice, they usually make the best one.
    b. So that children are given a choice, they usually make the best one.

12. a. We applied a sun-blocking lotion before going outdoors so that the midday sun wouldn't burn our skin.
    b. We applied a sun-blocking lotion before going outdoors unless the midday sun wouldn't burn our skin.

13. a. Telephone salespeople are annoying to me so that I'm polite to them.
    b. Telephone salespeople are annoying to me, though I'm usually polite to them.

14. a. Before memory typewriters were available, people had to retype whole pages in order to revise sentences.
    b. Before memory typewriters were available, people had to retype whole pages as much as revise sentences.

15. a. I don't like to eat corn unless I can get it fresh on the cob.
    b. I don't like to eat corn because I can get it fresh on the cob.

16. a. The coach let the youngster play, even though she didn't have as much experience as the older players.
    b. The coach let the youngster play, whereas she didn't have as much experience as the older players.

≡ Sentence Revising I

Review: The GED test asks you to select the best way to rewrite a sentence or to combine two
sentences. The next five sections will help you practice this skill. Whenever rewriting
sentences is required, the meaning of the new sentence must remain the same as before.
Always check your revised sentence for proper punctuation.
Example: I have a headache. I don't have time to lie down.
Although I have a headache, I don't have time to lie down now.

Directions: Combine the two sentences in each pair below using the part of the combined sentence
given in parentheses. Write the new sentence in the space provided.
Example: I want to quit smoking. I'm going to join a smoking cessation class.

(Since I) *Since I want to quit smoking, I'm going to join a*
smoking cessation class.

1. The mayor was under a lot of pressure. He had to act quickly. (Because the) _____

   _____

   _____

   _____

2. Bubba went to the Department of Public Safety office. He wanted to take the driver's license

   examination. (in order to) _____

   _____

   _____

3. The woman who provided the information was given the reward money. The information led to the

   conviction. (information which led) _____

   _____

   _____

   _____

4. We didn't have any hot water. The electricity that runs the water heater has been off since the storm.

   (water because) _____

   _____

   _____

5. I take enough time to assemble the ingredients. The recipe will be easy to prepare. (If I) _____

   _____

   _____

   _____

≋ Sentence Revising II

Directions: Rewrite each of the following sentences using the introductory words you are given. Check your sentence to be sure it restates the meaning of the original sentence. Always check a sentence for correct punctuation.

Example: Most people travel by car, but three million Americans a year travel by bus.

Even though *most people travel by car, three million Americans a year travel by bus.*

1. Swimming has traditionally been a popular recreational activity, but concern about safety keeps thousands of swimmers off the beaches.

   While swimming _____

   _____

   _____

2. Portable telephones can be used for business, home, and leisure, and are becoming widely popular.

   Because portable telephones _____

   _____

   _____

3. Cedar Point is the largest amusement park in America and is located in Sandusky, Ohio.

   The largest amusement park _____

   _____

   _____

4. Little Rock won't be able to open its municipal pools unless fifteen lifeguards are hired by May 30.

   If fifteen lifeguards are not _____

   _____

   _____

5. An increase in destructive, fatal fires in Idaho shows the public indifference to safety, reported the fire marshal.

   The fire marshal reported _____

   _____

   _____

6. The drummer in the rock band has taken a regular job, and he won't be available.

   Since _____

   _____

≡ Sentence Revising III

Directions: Choose the rewritten version (<u>a</u> or <u>b</u>) that best restates the meaning of the original sentence. Circle the letter of your choice.

1. The company that was responsible for the oil spill has been taken to court by the residents of the bay area in order to force the company to clean up the mess.

   a. The residents of the bay area are taking the company that was responsible for the oil spill to court in order to force the company to clean up the mess.

   b. The residents of the bay area that was responsible for the oil spill are taking the company to court in order to force them to clean up the mess.

2. Diners looking for low-cholesterol meals, and fast-food restaurants eager to cater to customer demand, are buying skinless, boneless chicken breasts as fast as producers can take them to market.

   a. Fast-food restaurants eager to cater to customer demand are buying skinless, boneless chicken breasts, and diners looking for low-cholesterol meals want them as fast as producers can take them to market.

   b. As fast as producers can take them to market, skinless, boneless chicken breasts are being bought by diners looking for low-cholesterol meals and by fast-food restaurants eager to cater to customer demand.

3. Medical waste represents less than one percent of beach litter; in fact, most trash is plastic, dropped by beachgoers themselves.

   a. Dropped by the beachgoers themselves, medical waste represents less than one percent of beach litter; in fact, most trash is plastic.

   b. While most trash is plastic, dropped by the beachgoers themselves, medical waste represents a little less than one percent of beach litter.

4. When choosing frozen desserts, most people want the rich taste of premium ice cream but want the lower calorie count of frozen yogurt.

   a. The lower calorie count of frozen yogurt, not the rich taste of premium ice cream, is what most people want when choosing frozen desserts.

   b. Most people want the lower calorie count of frozen yogurt, but they also want the rich taste of premium ice cream when choosing frozen desserts.

5. The unemployment service tries to match individuals who are looking for work with businesses that are in need of employees.

   a. Individuals who are looking for work are matched to businesses that are in need of employees by the unemployment service.

   b. Businesses that are in need of employees try to match individuals who are looking for work with the unemployment service.

6. Computers are replacing typewriters as the most standard piece of office equipment, and as a result secretaries are going back to school to learn how to use various computer software packages.

   a. Secretaries are going back to school to learn how to use various computer software packages, since computers are replacing typewriters as the most standard piece of office equipment.

   b. Secretaries are going back to school to learn how to use various computer software packages, although computers are replacing typewriters as the most standard piece of office equipment.

7. Military service has been, for many people, a path to a career in the service itself or training that can be applied later in civilian life.

   a. Many people have joined the military in order to have a service career or to receive job training for civilian life.

   b. Many people have joined the military whenever they have a service career or receive job training for civilian life.

Review: One special type of question on the GED Writing Skills Test requires you to choose the correct way to rewrite a sentence. The beginning of the new sentence is given. The exercise below gives you practice with the GED test format.

Directions: Choose the best answer to each item.

1. **Jerome is determined to stop drinking; in fact, he has started going to Alcoholics Anonymous meetings.**

   If you rewrote this sentence beginning with

   Because Jerome is determined to stop drinking,

   the next word should be

   (1) Alcoholics
   (2) started
   (3) going
   (4) he
   (5) meetings

2. **Adults can get free written information by calling the AIDS national hotline.**

   If you rewrote this sentence beginning with

   By calling the AIDS national hotline,

   the next word should be

   (1) information
   (2) can
   (3) adults
   (4) get
   (5) written

3. **He may never have seen a Porsche, but he's probably heard about that car.**

   If you rewrote this sentence beginning with

   Although he may never have seen a Porsche,

   the next word should be

   (1) he's
   (2) probably
   (3) heard
   (4) about
   (5) car

4. **Rick threw the empty pizza boxes on the floor, and he turned on the VCR to watch the movie he had rented.**

   If you rewrote this sentence beginning with

   Before he turned on the VCR to watch the movie he had rented,

   the next word should be

   (1) threw
   (2) boxes
   (3) pizza
   (4) the
   (5) Rick

5. **The neighborhood game room, where all the kids gather, has adults supervising the children at all times.**

   If you rewrote this sentence beginning with

   All the kids gather

   the next word should be

   (1) adults
   (2) the
   (3) times
   (4) at
   (5) room

6. **Many people take portable radios to the park, which angers the individuals who go to the park to enjoy the sights and sounds of nature.**

   If you rewrote this sentence beginning with

   The individuals who go to the park to enjoy the sights and sound of nature

   the next word should be

   (1) take
   (2) anger
   (3) are
   (4) many
   (5) radios

Review: Another type of GED test question will ask you the best way to combine two sentences. You will make a complete sentence using the words in the answer choices given. One choice should make more sense than the others. Repeated practice is important for you to master sentence revising.

Directions: Choose the <u>best answer</u> to each item.

1. **He owned a pair of Irish Setters. The dogs were his constant companions.**

   The most effective combination of these sentences would include which of the following groups of words?

   (1) Setters, but
   (2) Setters, thus,
   (3) The Irish Setters he owned
   (4) companions, he owned
   (5) a pair of dogs

2. **Jessie is the best cook in the family. Everyone says she should open a restaurant.**

   The most effective combination of these sentences would include which of the following groups of words?

   (1) family, although
   (2) family; in fact,
   (3) everyone who cooks
   (4) even if she is
   (5) restaurant, and everyone

3. **Penicillin is a commonly used antibiotic. There are some people who have a severe allergy to it.**

   The most effective combination of these sentences would include which of the following groups of words?

   (1) antibiotic, fortunately
   (2) The people who use antibiotics
   (3) antibiotic; however,
   (4) the antibiotic and its
   (5) antibiotic; and then

4. **The corner store has items that people need immediately. It is convenient because it is close to home.**

   The most effective combination of these sentences would include which of the following groups of words?

   (1) immediately, and it
   (2) immediately, but it
   (3) immediately, convenient
   (4) items close to
   (5) need because it

5. **The community was very small. It had one radio station that played only Big Band music from the 1930's.**

   The most effective combination of these sentences would include which of the following groups of words?

   (1) small; therefore,
   (2) small, and
   (3) small, but it
   (4) small, even though
   (5) small; and only

6. **The secretary decided to go home early. She had been feeling ill for the last two hours.**

   The most effective combination of these sentences would include which of the following groups of words?

   (1) early, and therefore
   (2) Since she had
   (3) early hours
   (4) secretary, she had
   (5) decided early to

Misplaced Modifiers

Review: Modifiers are words or phrases that limit or expand your understanding of another word or phrase. Sometimes a modifier is used in the wrong place.

Rule: Modifiers should be placed as near as possible to the word or words they modify in order to convey the meaning of a sentence clearly.

Incorrect: Mr. Morey explained how to work the microwave oven on the phone.

Correct: Mr. Morey explained on the phone how to work the microwave oven.

Directions: Some of the following sentences have misplaced modifiers; some sentences are correct as written. On another sheet of paper, rewrite the sentences below that contain misplaced modifiers, correcting the errors. Check the rewritten sentences for correct punctuation.

Example: There's a cup in the sink that's leaking.

There's a cup that's leaking in the sink.

1. My neighbor bought the used car from a reputable dealer with low mileage.

2. The plant supervisor discussed the possibility of implementing the employee medical coverage plan during lunch.

3. We discussed plans for the annual company picnic in the boss's office.

4. I returned the defective lawnmower to the store that I had bought.

5. In the blender, the chef's assistant mixed the ingredients for the cake filling.

6. Behind the secretary's desk, the janitor located the missing file.

7. Mr. Meyers yelled at the children who were playing in the street angrily.

8. Driving in the fog, the bus driver was unable to see the oncoming traffic.

9. The caseworker in the lobby with the beautiful long hair was explaining the application procedure to a client.

10. Destroyed by the fallen tree, Jorge looked sadly at the newly purchased car.

11. Jammed under the doorway, Mrs. Cheng found the missing lottery tickets.

12. Coming up the driveway on a skateboard, we waved to the smiling boy.

13. Containing over fifty-four software disks, Jennifer was cleaning out the file cabinet.

14. The painter began work on the rented house wearing overalls.

15. The Mississippi River has been polluted by factory waste which is over two miles wide.

16. Covered by the papers on the desk, we couldn't locate the keys to the computer room.

17. Mrs. Kaspar was waiting for her physician to call impatiently with the test results.

18. Wearing his full dress uniform, Jonathan was preparing for the arrival of the commander.

19. Disposing of the incriminating evidence, the police officers caught the bank manager who had been embezzling funds for years.

20. Elwin purchased a compact disc player from the audio store with seven special features.

21. Manufacturers are trying to produce a cigarette for smokers made of herbs.

22. Richard fed the cat before he left to play golf all afternoon.

23. Have you ever been bitten by fire ants working in the garden?

24. The building coming up on your left is the American Mutual Life building.

≡ Dangling Modifiers

Review: A dangling modifier does not have the object to which the modifier refers in the sentence.

Incorrect: Driving to Memphis, the highway was extremely crowded.

Who was driving to Memphis? The highway can't drive itself. The reader does not know who was driving to Memphis. The corrected sentence makes clear who was driving.

Correct: While we were driving to Memphis, the highway was extremely crowded.

Directions: Some of the following sentences contain a dangling modifier. Underline any dangling modifiers, and then write a correct form of that sentence on another piece of paper. Some of the sentences are correct as written.

Example: Barking joyfully, I greeted my dog.

I greeted my dog who was barking joyfully.

---

1. While enjoying lunch with my co-workers, my car was stolen.

2. Going to the hospital, the ambulance was hit by another car.

3. With time to spare, the printing crew finished the rush job.

4. At the age of thirteen, my family moved back East.

5. Walking home from the bus stop, the umbrella was caught by the wind and blew away.

6. The computer broke before I finished inputting the information.

7. Waiting for the check to arrive in the mail, the bills became overdue.

8. After working all day, the bed was a welcome sight.

9. Rushing to get to work, the flat tire on the car caused a delay.

10. While he was concentrating on the play-off game, his wife was preparing dinner.

11. Parking at the mall, my car was hit by a man who wasn't paying attention to what he was doing.

12. Wondering what to do next, the assembly line stopped while the supervisors discussed the problem.

13. Exhausted and sunburned, my trip would soon come to an end.

14. As the police were on the way to the accident, their own car was hit.

15. Walking through the discount store, the aisles were cluttered with merchandise.

16. Old and worn-out, the real estate agent showed us the big house.

17. Having read the recipe, a casserole was baked for the guests.

18. Speaking to a group of strangers, my knees knocked and my hands shook.

19. Before booking him, the thief was advised of his right to consult a lawyer.

20. While walking in the park, a huge dog bit my leg.

21. Reeling in the line quickly, the fish jumped off the hook.

22. After snooping around the office, the contract was found on a chair.

23. Dangling from the fishhook by its mouth, the excited boy reeled in his first fish.

24. Circling overhead, Jack watched the vultures hovering nearby.

25. Walking the dog around the block, it started to rain.

26. While cleaning out the attic, an old family photograph album was found.

27. Expensive and fancy, their friends took them to a new restaurant.

Unclear Pronoun Reference

Review: Some sentences contain pronouns that are confusing because the antecedent for the pronoun is unclear. When this happens, you should substitute the noun referred to for the unclear pronoun.

Incorrect: Writing helps them clarify their thinking.

Correct: Writing helps people clarify their thinking.

Directions: Each of the following sentences contains an unclear pronoun reference. Circle each unclear pronoun. Then rewrite each sentence, correcting any unclear pronouns.

Example: Maria and Rosa watched (her) TV.

Maria and Rosa watched Maria's TV.

1. Mrs. Hardin mentioned to Mrs. Mitchell that she could begin decorating the table for the buffet.

2. When employees and supervisors discuss safety conditions, they report what they think are the dangerous areas in the plant.

3. With rain and snow, it's hard to get around town.

4. Mr. Underling has been asking Jeremy to bring his money for the trip.

5. Discussing the incident, it was said that Ms. West was not responsible for her behavior.

6. On a regular basis, they broadcast news that is positive and enhances the community.

7. The Franklins invited some friends to the picnic, but they couldn't come.

Pronoun Reference in a Passage

Review: Sometimes in a passage pronouns are used to refer to objects or people mentioned several times. Make sure that each pronoun makes the meaning of a sentence and the whole passage clear.

Directions: Cross out any unclear pronouns in the following passage. Then rewrite the paragraph at the bottom of the page, correcting any unclear pronoun references.

After studying 6,000 families, two researchers have listed his or her characteristics of strong families. In strong families, there is a sense of commitment to it. Everyone knows that the family comes first. Work, friends, and possessions are second in importance to it. People in strong family units appreciate each other and look at the positive strengths of them. These families spend a great deal of time together doing things he or she likes. Strong families cope well with crises and stress. They solve problems among they in constructive ways that increase it. Good communication in which adults and children talk to each other freely is another characteristic of it. They become strong not by chance, but by design. By believing in each other and by working hard to build good relationships, every family can build its strength.

Rewritten paragraph:

_____

_____

_____

_____

_____

_____

_____

_____

_____

_____

_____

_____

_____

_____

_____

_____

Directions: Choose the <u>best answer</u> to each item.

Items 1–12 refer to the following paragraph.

(1) Remote control devices has become standard equipment in the electronic living room. (2) Some people have three remote control units, one each for their TV, videocassette recorder, and compact disc player, and "universal" remote control devices have been devised that enable you to control all of the electronic equipment with one unit. (3) All remotes work with infrared signals which is invisible. (4) When you press a button on the handheld device, a signal travels to the TV (or VCR, etc.), where a microprocessor receives it. (5) The microprocessor changes the signal into the type of command the TV receives when you work them manually. (6) Single remotes is ready for use as soon as you insert batteries. (7) "Universal" remotes must be programmed to make it compatible with all of your components. (8) Fortunately, this is a relatively simple task that don't require special tools. (9) For the convenience of a single remote unit, expect to pay from $60 to $200. (10) The more expensive units have extra functions and more streamlined technology. (11) Are these features worth the extra money them cost? (12) Judging by the rate at which "universal" remotes are selling there must be a large number of "couch potatoes" whom think so.

1. Sentence 1: **Remote control devices has become standard equipment in the electronic living room.**

   What correction should be made to this sentence?

   (1) replace <u>has</u> with <u>have</u>
   (2) replace <u>become</u> with <u>became</u>
   (3) change the spelling of <u>equipment</u> to equipmint
   (4) insert a comma after <u>equipment</u>
   (5) no correction is necessary

2. Sentence 2: **Some people have three remote control units, one each for their TV, videocassette recorder, and compact <u>disc player, and</u> "universal" remote control devices have been devised that enable you to control all of the electronic equipment with one unit.**

   Which of the following is the best way to write the underlined portion of this sentence? If you think the original is the best way, choose option (1).

   (1) disc player, and
   (2) disc player, even though
   (3) disc player. "Universal"
   (4) disc player; in addition
   (5) disc player; moreover

3. Sentence 3: **All remotes work with infrared <u>signals which is invisible.</u>**

   Which of the following is the best way to write the underlined portion of this sentence? If you think the original is the best way, choose option (1).

   (1) signals which is
   (2) signals; which is
   (3) signals; they are
   (4) signals which are
   (5) signals they're

4. Sentence 4: **When you press a button on the handheld device, a signal travels to the TV (or VCR, etc.), where a microprocessor receives it.**

   What correction should be made to this sentence?

   (1) replace <u>press</u> with <u>presses</u>
   (2) remove the comma after <u>device</u>
   (3) replace <u>where</u> with <u>when</u>
   (4) change the spelling of <u>receives</u> to <u>recieves</u>
   (5) no correction is necessary

5. Sentence 5: **The microprocessor changes the signal into the type of command the TV receives when you work them manually.**

What correction should be made to this sentence?

(1) replace changes with change
(2) change the spelling of signal to signel
(3) insert a comma after command
(4) replace them with it
(5) no correction is necessary

6. Sentence 6: **Single remotes is ready for use as soon as you insert batteries.**

Which of the following is the best way to write the underlined portion of this sentence? If you think the original is the best way, choose option (1).

(1) remote is ready
(2) remotes has been ready
(3) remotes was ready
(4) remotes are ready
(5) remotes have been ready

7. Sentence 7: **"Universal" remotes must be programmed to make it compatible with all of your components.**

What correction should be made to this sentence?

(1) insert a comma after programmed
(2) replace it with them
(3) replace with with from
(4) replace your with their
(5) no correction is necessary

8. Sentence 8: **Fortunately, this is a relatively simple task that don't require special tools.**

What correction should be made to this sentence?

(1) remove the comma after Fortunately
(2) replace is with was
(3) insert a comma after task
(4) replace don't with doesn't
(5) no correction is necessary

9. Sentence 9: **For the convenience of a single remote unit, expect to pay from $60 to $200.**

What correction should be made to this sentence?

(1) replace For with In spite of
(2) replace For with Since
(3) change the spelling of convenience to conveneince
(4) remove the comma after unit
(5) no correction is necessary

10. Sentence 10: **The more expensive units have extra functions and more streamlined technology.**

Which of the following is the best way to write the underlined portion of this sentence? If you think the original is the best way, choose option (1).

(1) have extra functions and more
(2) has more functions and extras
(3) used to have more functions and extras
(4) is using extra functions and more
(5) has used extra functions and more

11. Sentence 11: **Are these features worth the extra money them cost?**

What correction should be made to this sentence?

(1) replace these with it's
(2) replace these with there
(3) insert a comma after features
(4) replace them with they
(5) no correction is necessary

12. Sentence 12: **Judging by the rate at which "universal" remotes are selling, there must be a large number of "couch potatoes" whom think so.**

What correction should be made to this sentence?

(1) replace Judging with To judge
(2) insert a comma after rate
(3) change the spelling of potatoes to potatos
(4) replace whom with who
(5) no correction is necessary

Items 13–24 refer to the following paragraph.

(1) The old notion that crying can sometimes help you feel better may have a physical basis, according to the Tear Research Center in Minneapolis, the answer may lie in the tears themselves. (2) Chemicals often builds up during emotionally stressful times. (3) The gland that regulates tear secretion concentrates manganese and removes them. (4) Manganese, a mineral associated with mood swings. (5) Tears shed as a result of sadness, have a different chemical composition than those shed in response to an eye irritation. (6) Tears induced by the chemicals in onions stop wherever the chemicals are dissolved by the excess water. (7) Tears which are shed because of emotions, however, only stops when the tension has been released. (8) People who cry most often than others may have an overabundant supply of the emotional chemicals that are released during crying. (9) In fact, the tendency to cry under stress may be hereditary. (10) Doctors suggest that it may be better to listen to your body and crying it out when you're down in the dumps. (11) They say it's helpful to cry. (12) If you cry, your probably going to feel a lot better.

13. Sentence 1: **The old notion that crying can sometimes help you feel better may have a physical basis, according to the Tear Research Center in Minneapolis, the answer may lie in the tears themselves.**

Which of the following is the best way to write the underlined portion of this sentence? If you think the original is the best way, choose option (1).

(1) basis, according to
(2) basis; according to,
(3) basis; according to,
(4) basis, according to;
(5) basis. According to

14. Sentence 2: **Chemicals often builds up during emotionally stressful times.**

What correction should be made to this sentence?

(1) insert a comma after Chemicals
(2) replace builds with build
(3) change the spelling of emotionally to emotionaly
(4) insert a comma after emotionally
(5) no correction is necessary

15. Sentence 3: **The gland that regulates tear secretion concentrates manganese and removes them.**

What correction should be made to this sentence?

(1) replace regulates with regulate
(2) insert a comma after secretion
(3) replace concentrates with concentrate
(4) replace them with it
(5) no correction is necessary

16. Sentence 4: **Manganese, a mineral associated with mood swings.**

What correction should be made to this sentence?

(1) remove the comma after Manganese
(2) replace the comma with is
(3) change the spelling of associated to asociated
(4) replace associated with was associated
(5) no correction is necessary

17. Sentence 5: **Tears shed as a result of sadness, have a different chemical composition than those shed in response to an eye irritation.**

What correction should be made to this sentence?

(1) replace shed with shedded
(2) remove the comma after sadness
(3) replace have with has
(4) replace those with them
(5) no correction is necessary

18. Sentence 6: **Tears induced by the chemicals in onions stop wherever the chemicals are dissolved by the excess water.**

    Which of the following is the best way to write the underlined portion of this sentence? If you think the original is the best way, choose option (1).

    (1) stop wherever the
    (2) stop as soon as the
    (3) are stopped by the
    (4) having been stopped by the
    (5) is stopped by the

19. Sentence 7: **Tears which are shed because of emotions, however, only stops when the tension has been released.**

    What correction should be made to this sentence?

    (1) replace are with is
    (2) remove the comma after emotions
    (3) remove the comma after however
    (4) replace stops with stop
    (5) no correction is necessary

20. Sentence 8: **People who cry most often than others may have an overabundant supply of the emotional chemicals that are released during crying.**

    What correction should be made to this sentence?

    (1) replace cry with cries
    (2) replace most with more
    (3) replace others with anothers
    (4) insert a comma after chemicals
    (5) no correction is necessary

21. Sentence 9: **In fact, the tendency to cry under stress may be hereditary.**

    If you rewrote this sentence beginning with

    Crying under stress

    the next word should be

    (1) in
    (2) but
    (3) is
    (4) possibly
    (5) that

22. Sentence 10: **Doctors suggest that it may be better to listen to your body and crying it out when you're down in the dumps.**

    Which of the following is the best way to write the underlined portion of this sentence? If you think the original is the best way, choose option (1).

    (1) and crying it out
    (2) and having to cry it out
    (3) but crying it out
    (4) and cry it out
    (5) however, to cry it out

23. Sentence 11: **They say it's helpful to cry.**

    What correction should be made to this sentence?

    (1) insert quotation marks after say
    (2) replace it's with its
    (3) change the spelling of helpful to helpfull
    (4) replace to cry with crying
    (5) no correction is necessary

24. Sentence 12: **If you cry, your probably going to feel a lot better.**

    What correction should be made to this sentence?

    (1) replace cry with cried
    (2) replace your with you're
    (3) change the spelling of probably to probaly
    (4) change the spelling of a lot to alot
    (5) no correction is necessary

⟤ Simulated Test A

WRITING SKILLS, PART I

Directions

The Writing Skills Test is intended to measure your ability to use clear and effective English. It is a test of English as it should be written, not as it might be spoken.

This test consists of paragraphs with numbered sentences. Some of the sentences contain errors in sentence structure, usage, or mechanics (spelling, punctuation, and capitalization). After reading the numbered sentences, answer the multiple-choice items that follow. Some items refer to sentences that are correct as written. The best answer for these items is the one that leaves the sentences as originally written. The best answer for some items is the one that produces a sentence that is consistent with the verb tense and point of view used throughout the paragraph.

You will have 75 minutes for the multiple-choice items and 45 minutes for the essay. Work carefully, but do not spend too much time on any one item. Do not skip any items. Make a reasonable guess when you are not sure of an answer. You will not be penalized for incorrect answers.

When time is up, mark the last item you finished. This will tell you whether you can finish the real GED Test in the time allowed. Then complete the test. You may begin working on the second part of this test as soon as you complete the multiple-choice section.

Record your answers to the items on a copy of the answer sheet on page 109. Be sure that all required information is properly recorded on the answer sheet.

To record your answers, mark the numbered space on the answer sheet that corresponds to the answer you choose for each item on the test.

EXAMPLE:

Sentence 1: **We were all honored to meet governor Phillips.**

What correction should be made to this sentence?

(1)   insert a comma after <u>honored</u>
(2)   change the spelling of <u>honored</u> to <u>honered</u>
(3)   change <u>governor</u> to <u>Governor</u>
(4)   replace <u>were</u> with <u>was</u>
(5)   no correction is necessary   ① ② ● ④ ⑤

In this example, the word <u>governor</u> should be capitalized; therefore, answer space 3 would be marked on the answer sheet.

When you finish the test, use the Correlation Chart on page 76 to determine whether you are ready to take the real GED Test, and if not, which skill areas need additional review.

Do not rest the point of your pencil on the answer sheet while you are considering your answer. Make no stray or unnecessary marks. If you change an answer, erase your first mark completely. Mark only one answer space for each item; multiple answers will be scored as incorrect. Do not fold or crease your answer sheet.

Adapted with permission of the American Council on Education.

Directions: Choose the best answer to each item.

Items 1–9 refer to the following paragraph.

(1) Almost all electronic appliances, from microwave ovens to videocassette recorders, uses circuit boards. (2) The circuit boards contain the instruction panels, that tell machines what to do by conducting electrical current along pathways. (3) These boards were manufactured by using highly toxic acids to conduct electricity over copper-coated panels. (4) Although the boards are overused, the copper becomes overheated and stops the electrical current. (5) This is the most commonest cause of malfunctions in household appliances. (6) Researchers have been looking for a new way to manufacture circuit boards that would eliminate this here problem. (7) A new technology that uses an alloy ink to "print" the pathways are being tested. (8) An unexpected benifit of this new technology is that boards could be "printed" on fabrics and other flexible materials. (9) Medical devices that monitor heart rate or clothes that beam light could be "printed" on shirts, blouses, or dresses. (10) The application of this technology will only be limited by scientists' creativity.

1. Sentence 1: **Almost all electronic appliances, from microwave ovens to videocassette recorders, uses circuit boards.**

   What correction should be made to this sentence?

   (1) replace all with each
   (2) change the spelling of electronic to elecktronic
   (3) remove the comma after appliances
   (4) change uses to use
   (5) no correction is necessary

2. Sentence 2: **The circuit boards contain the instruction panels, that tell machines what to do by conducting electrical current along pathways.**

   What correction should be made to this sentence?

   (1) replace contain with contains
   (2) remove the comma after panels
   (3) replace tell with tells
   (4) insert a comma after current
   (5) no correction is necessary

3. Sentence 3: **These boards were manufactured by using highly toxic acids to conduct electricity over copper-coated panels.**

   Which of the following is the best way to write the underlined portion of this sentence? If you think the original is the best way, chose option (1).

   (1) were manufactured
   (2) are manufactured
   (3) is manufactured
   (4) has been manufactured
   (5) will be manufactured

4. Sentence 4: **Although the boards are overused, the copper becomes overheated and stops the electrical current.**

   Which of the following is the best way to write the underlined portion of this sentence? If you think the original is the best way, choose option (1).

   (1) Although the boards
   (2) The boards sometimes
   (3) The boards
   (4) Even if the boards
   (5) When the boards

5. Sentence 5: **This is the most commonest cause of malfunctions in household appliances.**

   What correction should be made to this sentence?

   (1) replace is with are
   (2) replace commonest with common
   (3) insert a comma after cause
   (4) change the spelling of appliances to apliances
   (5) no correction is necessary

6. Sentence 6: **Researchers have been looking for a new way to manufacture circuit boards that would eliminate this here problem.**

   What correction should be made to this sentence?

   (1) replace have with has
   (2) insert a comma after looking
   (3) replace that with who
   (4) remove here
   (5) no correction is necessary

7. Sentence 7: **A new technology that uses an alloy ink to "print" the pathways are being tested.**

   Which of the following is the best way to write the underlined portion of this sentence? If you think the original is the best way, choose option (1).

   (1) are being tested.
   (2) is being tested.
   (3) should have been tested.
   (4) have been tested.
   (5) were being tested.

8. Sentence 8: **An unexpected benifit of this new technology is that boards could be "printed" on fabrics and other flexible materials.**

   What correction should be made to this sentence?

   (1) change the spelling of benifit to benefit
   (2) replace is with was
   (3) insert a comma after boards
   (4) replace could be with should be
   (5) replace and with but

9. Sentence 10: **The application of this technology will only be limited by scientists' creativity.**

   If you rewrote this sentence beginning with

   Only scientists' creativity

   the next word should be

   (1) will
   (2) technology
   (3) application
   (4) by
   (5) limited

Items 10–19 refer to the following paragraph.

(1) Liquid protein diets promise obese Americans a way to take weight off faster. (2) No solid food eaten, but the dieter may drink up to five protein supplements per day. (3) These diets, which provide less than 800 calories a day should be undertaken only under proper medical supervision. (4) The average weight loss, according to doctors who use the diets to treat overweight patients, is about 60 pounds in 6 months. (5) The diet drinks are only available through hospital based programs where all patients' blood pressures, heart rates, and blood chemistries are checked at least twice a month to monitor his health condition. (6) There are some serious drawbacks to these diets. (7) A typical program costs at least $100 per week, bringing the total cost of the program to over $2,000. (8) The side effects can include fatigue, dry skin, diarrhea, chills, and muscle cramps. (9) All of them side effects are reversible once the patient starts eating again. (10) After the fast most programs are encouraging them to enter a maintenance phase for at least a year where they receive follow-up assistance to keep the weight off. (11) To be admitted to a program; a person generally has to be at least 40 pounds overweight. (12) It is crucial that individuals who are interested in a fasting diet check with there physician prior to beginning a program.

10. Sentence 1: **Liquid protein diets promise obese Americans a way to take weight off faster.**

What correction should be made to this sentence?

(1) replace promise with promises
(2) insert a comma after way
(3) replace take with taking
(4) replace faster with fast
(5) no correction is necessary

11. Sentence 2: **No solid food eaten, but the dieter may drink up to five protein supplements per day.**

Which of the following is the best way to write the underlined portion of this sentence? If you think the original is the best way, choose option (1).

(1) food eaten, but
(2) food are eaten, but
(3) food was eaten, but
(4) food is eaten, but
(5) food has been eaten, but

12. Sentence 3: **These diets, which provide less than 800 calories a day should be undertaken only under proper medical supervision.**

What correction should be made to this sentence?

(1) insert a comma after day
(2) replace should be with has been
(3) replace undertaken with undertook
(4) change the spelling of medical to medicle
(5) no correction is necessary

13. Sentence 5: **The diet drinks are only available through hospital based programs where all patients' blood pressures, heart rates, and blood chemistries are checked at least twice a month to monitor his health condition.**

What correction should be made to this sentence?

(1) replace are with was
(2) replace patients' with patient's
(3) remove the comma after pressures
(4) replace his with their
(5) change the spelling of health to helath

14. Sentences 6 and 7: **There are some serious drawbacks to these diets. A typical program costs at least $100 per week, bringing the total cost of the program to over $2,000.**

The most effective combination of sentence 6 and 7 would include which of the following groups of words?

(1) Since there are some serious drawbacks
(2) Although there is one drawback
(3) diets; for example, a typical program
(4) and so a typical program costs
(5) but, a typical program costs

15. Sentence 8: **The side effects can include fatigue, dry skin, diarrhea, chills, and muscle cramps.**

What correction should be made to this sentence?

(1) replace can include with includes
(2) insert a comma after include
(3) remove the comma after fatigue
(4) change the spelling of muscle to mucsle
(5) no correction is necessary

16. Sentence 9: **All of them side effects are reversible once the patient starts eating again.**

What correction should be made to this sentence?

(1) replace them with these
(2) replace are with is
(3) insert a comma after reversible
(4) replace starts with starting
(5) no correction is necessary

17. Sentence 10: **After the fast, most programs are encouraging them to enter a maintenance phase for at least a year where they receive follow-up assistance to keep the weight off.**

What correction should be made to this sentence?

(1) remove the comma after fast
(2) replace are with is
(3) replace them with dieters
(4) change the spelling of assistance to assistence
(5) no correction is necessary

18. Sentence 11: **To be admitted to a program; a person generally has to be at least 40 pounds overweight.**

Which of the following is the best way to write the underlined portion of this sentence? If you think the original is the best way, choose option (1).

(1) program; a person
(2) program. A person
(3) program, but a person
(4) program, a person
(5) program, although a person

19. Sentence 12: **It is crucial that individuals who are interested in a fasting diet check with there physician prior to beginning a program.**

What correction should be made to this sentence?

(1) insert a comma after crucial
(2) insert a comma after diet
(3) replace there with their
(4) change the spelling of physician to physican
(5) no correction is necessary

Items 20–29 refer to the following paragraph.

(1) To get results from companys that sell defective products, a written letter of complaint is more effective than a phone call. (2) Letters that generally gets responses include the following components. (3) Begin the letter with a clear statement that specifically describes the problem and to express the dissatisfaction. (4) Next, include a statement of what you expected the company to do. (5) Specify weather a refund, a credit, or a replacement is desired. (6) Its your responsibility to tell the company officers how they can satisfy your request. (7) If you tell them you will never buy another product from the company, they may not feel it necessary to resolve the current problem. (8) Therefore, include a statement that indicates that you will continue to purchase goods from the company if they satisfies your request. (9) Close by requesting a speedy resolution and state that you have included a proof of purchase. (10) To write effective letters of complaint will often resolve your problem in the most expeditious manner.

20. Sentence 1: **To get results from companys that sell defective products, a written letter of complaint is more effective than a phone call.**

    What correction should be made to this sentence?

    (1) change the spelling of companys to companies
    (2) remove the comma after products
    (3) replace is with are
    (4) replace more with most
    (5) no correction is necessary

21. Sentence 2: **Letters that generally gets responses include the following components.**

    What correction should be made to this sentence?

    (1) replace that with who
    (2) replace gets with get
    (3) insert a comma after responses
    (4) replace include with includes
    (5) no correction is necessary

22. Sentence 3: **Begin the letter with a clear statement that specifically describes the problem and to express your dissatisfaction.**

    Which of the following is the best way to write the underlined portion of this sentence? It you think the original is the best, choose option (1).

    (1) and to express your
    (2) and expressing your
    (3) but to express your
    (4) and expresses your
    (5) and expressed your

23. Sentence 4: **Next, include a statement of what you expected the company to do.**

    Which of the following is the best way to write the underlined portion of this sentence? If you think the original is the best way, choose option (1).

    (1) you expected
    (2) you've expected
    (3) you will expect
    (4) you expect
    (5) you is expecting

24. Sentence 5: **Specify weather a refund, a credit, or a replacement is desired.**

What correction should be made to this sentence?

(1) replace <u>weather</u> with <u>whether</u>
(2) remove the comma after <u>refund</u>
(3) replace <u>or</u> with <u>and</u>
(4) replace <u>is</u> with <u>are</u>
(5) no correction is necessary

25. Sentence 6: **Its your responsibility to tell the company officers how they can satisfy your request.**

What correction should be made to this sentence?

(1) replace <u>Its</u> with <u>It's</u>
(2) change the spelling of <u>responsibility</u> to <u>responsability</u>
(3) insert a comma after <u>officers</u>
(4) replace <u>satisfy</u> with <u>satisfied</u>
(5) replace <u>your</u> with <u>you're</u>

26. Sentence 7: **If you tell them you will never buy another product from the <u>company, they may not feel</u> it necessary to resolve the current problem.**

Which of the following is the best way to write the underlined portion of this sentence? If you think the original is the best way, choose option (1).

(1) company, they may not feel
(2) company. They may not feel
(3) company; they may not feel
(4) company; they, may not feel
(5) company. But then they might not feel

27. Sentence 8: **Therefore, include a statement that indicates that you will continue to purchase goods from the company if they satisfies your request.**

What correction should be made to this sentence?

(1) remove the comma after <u>Therefore</u>
(2) replace <u>indicates</u> with <u>indicated</u>
(3) insert a comma after <u>goods</u>
(4) replace <u>satisfies</u> with <u>satisfy</u>
(5) no correction is necessary

28. Sentence 9: **Close by requesting a speedy resolution and state that you have included a proof of purchase.**

If you rewrote sentence 9 beginning with

<u>In your closing statement,</u>

the next words should be

(1) resolution and statement
(2) included are
(3) request a
(4) proof of purchase
(5) faulty

29. Sentence 10: **<u>To write</u> effective letters of complaint will often resolve your problem in the most expeditious manner.**

Which of the following is the best way to write the underlined portion of this sentence? If you think the original is the best way, choose option (1)

(1) To write
(2) In order to write
(3) Having to write
(4) Writing
(5) Having written

Items 30–39 refer to the following paragraph.

(1) Many people who grow vegetable gardens to increase the quality of the produce their families consume. (2) Other reasons people are attracted to backyard gardening. (3) These reasons include the convenience of having fresh vegetables close at hand and the savings accrued by growing their own food. (4) The vegetables you choose to grow should be the ones your family likes the best and use most often. (5) Contrary to popular belief, it do not take much space to grow a few vegetables. (6) Even an apartment dweller can grow most of their own fresh produce in tubs or window gardens. (7) After the initial soil preparation and planting, gardens only need weekly weeding and watering in order to thrive until the plants are ready to be harvested. (8) Some plants such as tomatoes, peppers, squash, and cucumbers will continue to produce the entire Summer. (9) Other plants such as peas, radishes, green beans, and corn will produce a large harvest only within one or two weeks during the season. (10) It's important to think ahead about what you will do with the extra produce that is harvested during this short time span. (11) Surplus vegetables can be frozen or put into cans to provide low-cost food year-round from the garden. (12) Growing flavorful produce for family consumption continues to be a favorite hobby of many people.

30. Sentence 1: **Many people who grow vegetable gardens to increase the quality of the produce their families consume.**

    What correction should be made to this sentence?

    (1) remove who
    (2) insert a comma after gardens
    (3) change the spelling of families to familys
    (4) replace consume with consumes
    (5) no correction is necessary

31. Sentences 2 and 3: **Other reasons people are attracted to backyard gardening. These reasons include the convenience of having fresh vegetables close at hand and the savings accrued by growing their own food.**

    The most effective combination of sentence 2 and 3 would include which of the following groups of words?

    (1) reasons do not include
    (2) vegetables include
    (3) gardening is that the
    (4) gardening include the
    (5) therefore, it includes

32. Sentence 4: **The vegetables you choose to grow should be the ones that your family likes the best and use most often.**

    What correction should you make to this sentence?

    (1) replace choose with chose
    (2) replace ones with one
    (3) insert comma after best
    (4) replace use with uses
    (5) replace often. with often?

33. Sentence 5: **Contrary to popular belief, it do not take much space to grow a few vegetables.**

    Which of the following is the best way to write the underlined portion of this sentence? If you think the original is the best way, choose option (1).

    (1) do not take
    (2) will not take
    (3) does not take
    (4) has not taken
    (5) have not taken

34. Sentence 6: **Even an apartment dweller can grow most of their own fresh produce in tubs or window gardens.**

What correction should be made to this sentence?

(1) replace grow with have grown
(2) insert a comma after grow
(3) replace their with his or her
(4) insert a comma after produce
(5) no correction is necessary

35. Sentence 7: **After the initial soil preparation and planting, gardens only need weekly weeding and watering in order to thrive until the plants are ready to be harvested.**

What correction should be made to this sentence?

(1) change the spelling of preparation to preparetion
(2) remove the comma after planting
(3) replace thrive with thriving
(4) replace are with is
(5) no correction is necessary

36. Sentence 8: **Some plants such as tomatoes, peppers, squash, and cucumbers will continue to produce the entire Summer.**

What correction should be made to this sentence?

(1) change the spelling of tomatoes to tomatos
(2) replace continue with continues
(3) insert a comma after produce
(4) replace Summer with summer
(5) no correction is necessary

37. Sentence 9: **Other plants such as peas, radishes, green beans, and corn will produce a large harvest only within one or two weeks during the season.**

Which of the following is the best way to write the underlined portion of this sentence? If you think the original is the best way, choose option (1).

(1) will produce a large harvest only
(2) will produce a large only harvest
(3) produces the largest harvest only
(4) produced a large harvest only
(5) will only produce a large harvest

38. Sentence 10: **It's important to think ahead about what you will do with the extra produce that is harvested during this short time span.**

What correction should be made to this sentence?

(1) replace It's with Its
(2) insert a comma after ahead
(3) replace is with are
(4) insert a comma after harvested
(5) no correction is necessary

39. Sentence 11. **Surplus vegetables can be frozen or put into cans to provide low-cost food year-round from the garden.**

Which of the following is the best way to write the underlined portion of this sentence? If you think the original is the best way, choose option (1).

(1) or put into cans
(2) or be put into cans
(3) or tried to be canned
(4) or canned
(5) or will be put into cans

Items 40–48 refer to the following paragraph.

(1) Kawasaki Syndrome is leading the cause of acquired heart disease among children in the United States. (2) Named after the pediatrician who reported the first case in 1967, Kawasaki Syndrome is caused by a viral infecktion that can trigger heart damage. (3) Most victims are between one and two years old. (4) Asian and African American children appear to be more susceptible than Caucasian children. (5) Boys are more susceptible than girls. (6) The illness does not appear to be contagious but scientists are not positive that it cannot be transmitted. (7) Most children who develop Kawasaki Syndrome exhibit their symptoms within a month of a carpet being cleaned in the home. (8) The Centers for Disease Control recommend that children especially those under five, be kept away from freshly shampooed carpets for at least a day. (9) Parents were also advised not to clean rugs between November and May, the months when most Kawasaki cases appear. (10) Doctors suspect that a virus carried by dust mites are responsible for this bizarre illness. (11) The symptoms of Kawasaki Syndrome are fever, deep rash, swollen palms and soles, red lips and tongue, and bloodshot eyes. (12) Quick diagnosis and treatment increases the chances of avoiding complications.

40. Sentence 1: **Kawasaki Syndrome is leading the cause of acquired heart disease among children in the United States.**

Which of the following is the best way to write the underlined portion of this sentence? If you think the original is the best way, choose option (1).

(1) is leading the cause of
(2) were the leading cause of
(3) causes many
(4) is the leading cause of
(5) caused

41. Sentence 2: **Named after the pediatrician who reported the first case in 1967, Kawasaki Syndrome is caused by a viral infecktion that can trigger heart damage.**

What correction should be made to this sentence?

(1) replace reported with reports
(2) remove the comma after 1967
(3) replace is with are
(4) change the spelling of infecktion to infection
(5) insert a comma after infecktion

42. Sentences 3 and 4: **Most victims are between one and two years old. Asian and African American children appear to be more susceptible than Caucasian children.**

Which of the following is the best way to write the underlined portion of these sentences? If you think the original is the best way, choose option (1).

(1) old. Asian
(2) old; but, Asian
(3) old, so Asian
(4) old; therefore Asian
(5) old, however, Asian

43. Sentence 6: **The illness does not appear to be contagious but scientists are not positive that it cannot be transmitted.**

What correction should be made to this sentence?

(1) replace does with do
(2) insert a comma after contagious
(3) change scientists to scientist's
(4) replace are with is
(5) no correction is necessary

44. Sentence 7: **Most children who develop Kawasaki Syndrome exhibit their symptoms within a month of a carpet being cleaned in the home.**

If you rewrote sentence 7 beginning with

The symptoms of Kawasaki Syndrome that children exhibit

the next words should be

(1) usually begin within
(2) most of them are
(3) are cleaned in the carpet
(4) has been within
(5) is likely to have begun

45. Sentence 8: **The Centers for Disease Control recommend that children especially those under five, be kept away from freshly shampooed carpets for at least a day.**

Which of the following is the best way to write the underlined portion of this sentence? If you think the original is the best way, choose option (1).

(1) children especially those under five,
(2) children, especially those under five,
(3) children, especially those under five
(4) children; especially those under five,
(5) children, especially those under five;

46. Sentence 9: **Parents were also advised not to clean rugs between November and May, the months when most Kawasaki cases appear.**

Which of the following is the best way to write the underlined portion of this sentence? If you think the original is the best way, choose option (1).

(1) were also advised
(2) are also advised
(3) was also advised
(4) also been advised
(5) has also been advised

47. Sentence 10: **Doctors suspect that a virus carried by dust mites are responsible for this bizarre illness.**

What correction should be made to this sentence?

(1) replace suspect with suspects
(2) insert a comma after virus
(3) replace are with is
(4) change the spelling of responsible to responsable
(5) no correction is necessary

48. Sentence 12: **Quick diagnosis and treatment increases the chances of avoiding complications.**

What corrections should be made to this sentence?

(1) insert a comma after diagnosis
(2) replace increases with increase
(3) replace chances of with chance to
(4) insert a comma after chances
(5) no correction is necessary

Items 49–55 refer to the following paragraph.

(1) Communication between a homeowner and a contractor is important when home improvement projects were planned. (2) The Council of Better Business Bureaus suggests that a homeowner choose a bonded, lisenced, or insured contractor. (3) To protect yourself, verify the credentials of the contractor. (4) And talk with some of the contractor's previous customers. (5) The terms of agreement should be specified in a written contract. (6) The contract should give complete financial information and specifying the quality and type of materials to be used. (7) Contracts also usually include any warranties on the work performed or the materials used. (8) Always take time to think over a contract before signing. (9) This is a way to avoid high-pressure sales tactics. (10) Inspect the contractor's work and negotiate any disagreements before making payment. (11) Following these guidelines will help protect you and ensure that the remodeling project is done to your satisfaction.

49. Sentence 1: **Communication between a homeowner and a contractor is important when home improvement projects were planned.**

Which of the following is the best way to write the underlined portion of this sentence? If you think the original is the best way, chose option (1).

(1) when home improvement projects were planned.
(2) if you have planned home improvement projects.
(3) when planning home improvement projects.
(4) because of planning home improvement projects.
(5) although home improvement projects will be planned.

50. Sentence 2: **The Council of Better Business Bureaus suggests that a homeowner choose a bonded, lisenced, or insured contractor.**

What correction should be made to this sentence?

(1) insert a comma after Bureaus
(2) replace suggests with suggest
(3) remove the comma after bonded
(4) change the spelling of lisenced to licensed
(5) insert a comma after insured

51. Sentences 3 and 4: **To protect yourself, verify the credentials of the contractor. And talk with some of the contractor's previous customers.**

Which of the following is the best way to write the underlined portion of these sentences? If you think the original is the best way, choose option (1).

(1) contractor. And talk
(2) contractor; and, talk
(3) contractor and talk
(4) contractor, and, talk
(5) contractor, and talk

52. Sentence 6: **The contractor should give complete financial information and specifying the quality and type of materials to be used.**

Which of the following is the best way to write the underlined portion of this sentence? If you think the original is the best way, choose option (1).

(1) information and specifying
(2) information, however specifying
(3) information although to specify
(4) information; but specifying
(5) information and specify

53. Sentence 7: **Contracts also usually include any warranties on the work performed or the materials used.**

If you rewrote this sentence beginning with

Any warranties on the work performed or the materials used

the next words should be

(1) are usually included
(2) is included
(3) has included
(4) was included
(5) has been usually included

54. Sentences 8 and 9: **Always take time to think over a contract before signing. This is a way to avoid high-pressure sales tactics.**

The most effective combination of these sentences would include which of the following groups or words?

(1) Tactics to avoid
(2) To avoid contract signing
(3) Taking time to think over
(4) signing, unfortunately
(5) When high-pressure sales tactics are avoided

55. Sentence 10: **Inspect the contractor's work and negotiate any disagreements before making payment.**

What correction should be made to this sentence?

(1) replace Inspect with Inspecting
(2) replace contractor's with contractors
(3) insert a comma after negotiate
(4) insert a comma after disagreements
(5) no correction is necessary

Answers are on page 102.

 # Simulated Test A

WRITING SKILLS, PART II
Directions

Part II of the Writing Skills Test determines how well you write. You will have 45 minutes to write an essay that explains or presents an opinion or states a view on an issue. Follow these steps:

1. Carefully read the directions and the essay topic below.

2. Plan your essay before you write. Stick to the topic.

3. Use scratch paper to make notes.

4. Write your essay on a copy of the answer sheet on page 110. Write legibly and use a ballpoint pen so that your evaluator will be able to read your writing.

5. Read what you have written, and make any changes that will improve your essay.

6. Check your essay for sentence structure, spelling, punctuation, capitalization, and usage. Make any necessary corrections.

Topic

Thousands of Americans are killed with handguns each year. Many people die as a result of accidents while handling the guns, and others are shot during domestic arguments. Many citizens are now proposing a ban on handguns.

Write a composition of about 200 words, stating your opinion about whether tougher gun control is needed. You may support or oppose gun control. Use specific examples to support your argument.

Model answer and correction instructions are on pages 104 and 108.

Adapted with permission of the American Council on Education.

≡ Analysis of Performance: Writing Skills Simulated Test A

Name: _____ Class: _____ Date: _____

Part I

The chart below will help you determine your strengths and weaknesses in grammar usage, sentence structure, and mechanics (spelling, capitalization, and punctuation).

Directions

Circle the number of each item that you answered correctly on the Simulated GED Test A. Count the number of items you answered correctly in each column. Write the amount in the Total Correct space of each column. (For example, if you answered 13 Mechanics items correctly, place the number 13 in the blank before out of 13). Complete this process for the remaining columns.

Count the number of items you answered correctly in each row. Write that amount in the Total Correct space of each row. (For example, in the Construction Shift row, write the number correct in the blank before out of 7). Complete this process for the remaining rows.

Test A Analysis of Performance Chart

Item Types:	Mechanics (Unit 1)	Usage (Unit 2)	Sentence Structure (Unit 3)	Total Correct
Construction Shift		28, 53	9, 14, 31, 44	_____ out of 6
Sentence Correction	2, 8, 12, 15, 20, 25, 36, 38, 41, 43, 50	1, 5, 6, 10, 16, 19, 21, 24, 27, 32, 47, 48, 55	13, 17, 34	_____ out of 27
Sentence Revision	18, 45	3, 7, 23, 29, 33, 40, 46, 49, 54	4, 11, 22, 26, 30, 35, 37, 39, 42, 51, 52	_____ out of 22
Total Correct	_____ out of 13	_____ out of 24	_____ out of 18	Total Correct: _____ out of 55 1–40 = You need more review 41–55 = Congratulations! You're ready

If you answered fewer than 41 of the 55 items correctly, determine which areas are hardest for you. Go back to the *Steck-Vaughn GED Writing Skills* book and review the content in those specific areas.

In the parentheses under the heading, the unit numbers tell you where you can find the beginning of specific instruction about that area of grammar in the *Steck-Vaughn GED Writing Skills* book. Also refer to the chart on page 3.

Part II

Have your instructor or another person read and score your essay. Essays are scored on a scale of * to 6, with * the lowest score and 6 the highest score. Follow the instructions on page 108.

Enter the reader's score here _____

Ask the reader to help you determine the strong points of the essay and areas where the essay needs improvement. The feedback you receive from the reader will help you improve the next essay you write.

WRITING SKILLS, PART I

Directions

The Writing Skills Test is intended to measure your ability to use clear and effective English. It is a test of English as it should be written, not as it might be spoken.

This test consists of paragraphs with numbered sentences. Some of the sentences contain errors in sentence structure, usage, or mechanics (spelling, punctuation, and capitalization). After reading the numbered sentences, answer the multiple-choice items that follow. Some items refer to sentences that are correct as written. The best answer for these items is the one that leaves the sentences as originally written. The best answer for some items is the one that produces a sentence that is consistent with the verb tense and point of view used throughout the paragraph.

You will have 75 minutes for the multiple-choice items and 45 minutes for the essay. Work carefully, but do not spend too much time on any one item. Do not skip any items. Make a reasonable guess when you are not sure of an answer. You will not be penalized for incorrect answers.

When time is up, mark the last item you finished. This will tell you whether you can finish the real GED Test in the time allowed. Then complete the test. You may begin working on the second part of this test as soon as you complete the multiple-choice section.

Record your answers to the items on a copy of the answer sheet on page 109. Be sure that all required information is properly recorded on the answer sheet.

To record your answers, mark the numbered space on the answer sheet that corresponds to the answer you choose for each item on the test.

EXAMPLE:

Sentence 1: **We were all honored to meet governor Phillips.**

What correction should be made to this sentence?

(1)   insert a comma after honored
(2)   change the spelling of honored to honered
(3)   change governor to Governor
(4)   replace were with was
(5)   no correction is necessary

In this example, the word governor should be capitalized; therefore, answer space 3 would be marked on the answer sheet.

When you finish the test, use the Correlation Chart on page 91 to determine whether you are ready to take the real GED Test, and if not, which skill areas need additional review.

Do not rest the point of your pencil on the answer sheet while you are considering your answer. Make no stray or unnecessary marks. If you change an answer, erase your first mark completely. Mark only one answer space for each item; multiple answers will be scored as incorrect. Do not fold or crease your answer sheet.

Directions: Choose the best answer to each item.

Items 1–10 refer to the following paragraph.

   (1) Each year the staffs of hospital emergancy rooms treat more than 25 million children who are in distress. (2) The most common reasons children are taken to hospitals are trauma (an injury or accident), infectious disease (such as the flu), or a chronic illness (such as asthma). (3) Whenever a child is taken to the hospital; the experience can be as frightening for the parent as for the child. (4) It is important to try to remain calm in order to make appropriate decisions regarding your child's care. (5) Often hospitals encourage them to stay with their children to provide emotional support. (6) Until you are anxious, you need to focus on the child's need to be reassured. (7) Kids take cues from their parents on how to react to situations. (8) If you're hysterical, your child may become more frightened from your reaction than from his or her actual discomfort. (9) Try not to contribute to your child's fear. (10) Talk to your child in a soft voice, and explain that what is happening to them will soon be over. (11) Your participation will help the hospital staff treat your child more quickly and safely. (12) No parent wants to think of his or her children becoming sick or injured, but when they are, a parent can be the most helpful by remaining calm.

1. Sentence 1: **Each year the staffs of hospital emergency rooms treat more than 25 million children who are in distress.**

   What correction should be made to this sentence?

   (1) change the spelling of emergancy to emergency
   (2) replace treat with treats
   (3) insert a comma after treat
   (4) replace children with children's
   (5) replace who with whom

2. Sentence 2: **The most common reasons children are taken to hospitals are trauma (an injury or accident), infectious disease (such as the flu), or a chronic illness (such as asthma).**

   What correction should be made to this sentence?

   (1) replace most with more
   (2) insert a comma after children
   (3) replace hospitals with hospitals'
   (4) remove the comma after accident
   (5) no correction is necessary

3. Sentence 3: **Whenever a child is taken to the hospital; the experience can be as frightening for the parent as for the child.**

   Which of the following is the best way to write the underlined portion of this sentence? If you think the original is the best way, choose option (1).

   (1) the hospital; the
   (2) the hospital, the
   (3) the hospital, even though
   (4) the hospital; until
   (5) the hospital; if

4. Sentence 4: **It is important to try to remain calm in order to make appropriate decisions regarding your child's care.**

   If you rewrote this sentence beginning with

   Remaining calm

   the next word should be

   (1) children
   (2) try
   (3) decisions
   (4) important
   (5) is

5. Sentence 5: **Often hospitals encourage them to stay with their children to provide emotional support.**

   What correction should be made to this sentence?

   (1) insert a comma after Often
   (2) replace encourage with encourages
   (3) replace them with parents
   (4) insert a comma after children
   (5) no correction is necessary

6. Sentence 6: **Until you are anxious, you need to focus on the child's need to be reassured.**

   Which of the following is the best way to write the underlined portion of this sentence? If you think the original is the best way, choose option (1).

   (1) Until you are anxious, you
   (2) Although you are anxious, you
   (3) Being anxious, you
   (4) Overcoming anxiousness, you
   (5) If you are anxious, you

7. Sentences 7 and 8: **Kids take cues from their parents on how to react to situations. If you're hysterical, your child may become more frightened from your reaction than from his or her actual discomfort.**

   The most effective combination of sentences 7 and 8 would include which of the following groups of words?

   (1) parents may be hysterical
   (2) situations, like if
   (3) situations; but
   (4) situations; for example, if
   (5) a hysterical reaction to

8. Sentence 10: **Talk to your child in a soft voice, and explain that what is happening to them will soon be over.**

   What correction should be made to this sentence?

   (1) replace in with by
   (2) insert a semicolon after voice
   (3) replace is with are
   (4) replace them with him or her
   (5) no correction is necessary

9. Sentence 11: **Your participation will help the hospital staff treat your child more quickly and safely.**

   What correction should be made to this sentence?

   (1) replace Your with You're
   (2) insert a comma after staff
   (3) replace treat with treats
   (4) remove more
   (5) replace safely with safer

10. Sentence 12: **No parent wants to think of his or her children becoming sick or injured, but when they are, a parent can be the most helpful by remaining calm.**

    Which of the following is the best way to write the underlined portion of this sentence? If you think the original is the best way, choose option (1).

    (1) injured, but
    (2) being injured, but
    (3) having been injured, but
    (4) injured, unless
    (5) injured; unless

Items 11–19 refer to the following paragraph.

(1) Barbecued foods are becoming increasingly popular. (2) Whether it is in the back yard, at the beach, and on an apartment balcony, barbecuing is an easy way to prepare food. (3) In addition to the traditional steaks, hamburgers, and chicken, cooks are putting fish, vegetables and cooking breads on a grill. (4) The wonderful smoky barbecue flavor can be enhanced by adding different kinds of wood. (5) The most popular are mesquite and hickory. (6) Before adding wood chunks or chips, soak it in water for at least twenty minutes. (7) Then toss the wood onto the hot fire just minutes before placing food on the grill. (8) Other barbecue fanatics throw grapevines and herbs that lend subtle flavors to grilled food on the glowing coals. (9) Most barbecue grills have hot spots, so its best to trim all excess fat from meats. (10) There will be less flareup and smoke if meats is well-trimmed. (11) Vegetables and breads, be grilled over lower heat. (12) Making an entire meal on a barbecue grill is a cooking method that has been used for centurys.

11. Sentence 2: **Whether it is in the back yard, at the beach, and on an apartment balcony, barbecuing is an easy way to prepare food.**

    What correction should be made to this sentence?

    (1) remove the comma after yard
    (2) replace and with or
    (3) remove the comma after balcony
    (4) replace is with has been
    (5) no correction is necessary

12. Sentence 3: **In addition to the traditional steaks, hamburgers, and chicken, cooks are putting fish, vegetables and cooking breads on a grill.**

    Which of the following is the best way to write the underlined portion of this sentence? If you think the original is the best way, choose option (1).

    (1) fish, vegetables, and cooking breads
    (2) fish, cooking vegetables, and breads
    (3) fish, vegetables, and breads
    (4) fish and also cooking vegetables and breads
    (5) fish, vegetables and having cooked bread

13. Sentences 4 and 5: **The wonderful smoky barbecue flavor can be enhanced by adding different kinds of wood. The most popular are mesquite and hickory.**

    The most effective combination of sentences 4 and 5 would include which of the following groups of words?

    (1) barbecue flavors of wood
    (2) woods being popular
    (3) wood; otherwise the
    (4) wood; in fact, the
    (5) wood; however,

14. Sentence 6: **Before adding wood chunks or chips, soak it in water for at least twenty minutes.**

    What correction should be made to this sentence?

    (1) replace Before with While
    (2) remove the comma after chips
    (3) replace it with them
    (4) insert a comma after water
    (5) no correction is necessary

15. Sentence 8: **Other barbecue fanatics throw <u>grapevines and herbs that lend</u> subtle flavors to grilled food onto the glowing coals.**

Which of the following is the best way to write the underlined portion of this sentence? If you think the original is the best way, choose option (1).

(1) grapevines and herbs that lend
(2) grapevines that lend, and herbs, too
(3) herbs that lend with grapevines
(4) herbs and grapevines having lent
(5) grapevines, herbs, and those that lend

16. Sentence 9: **Most barbecue grills have hot spots, so its best to trim all excess fat from meats.**

What correction should be made to this sentence?

(1) replace <u>have</u> with <u>has</u>
(2) replace <u>its</u> with <u>it's</u>
(3) insert a comma after <u>trim</u>
(4) insert a comma after <u>fat</u>
(5) no correction is necessary

17. Sentence 10: **There will be less flareup and <u>smoke if meats is</u> well-trimmed.**

Which of the following is the best way to write the underlined portion of this sentence? If you think the original is the best way, choose option (1).

(1) smoke, if meats is
(2) smoke if meats are
(3) smoke, unless meats is
(4) smoke, unless meats are
(5) smoke and if meats are

18. Sentence 11: **Vegetables and <u>breads, be grilled over</u> lower heat.**

Which of the following is the best way to write the underlined portion of this sentence? If you think the original is the best way, choose option (1).

(1) breads, be grilled over
(2) breads, having been grilled over
(3) breads has been grilled over
(4) breads should be grilled over
(5) breads is grilled over

19. Sentence 12: **Making an entire meal on a barbecue grill is a cooking method that has been used for centurys.**

What correction should be made to this sentence?

(1) replace <u>entire</u> with <u>entyre</u>
(2) insert a comma after <u>grill</u>
(3) replace <u>is</u> with <u>are</u>
(4) insert a comma after <u>method</u>
(5) replace <u>centurys</u> with <u>centuries</u>

Items 20–29 refer to the following paragraph.

(1) Across the country, popcorn a favorite low-calorie snack. (2) Americans buy over 800 million pounds of unpopped popcorn each year. (3) According to the Popcorn Institute located in Chicago. (4) Two Brothers from Texas have developed a new variety of popcorn. (5) Called popcorn-on-the-cob, a new food fad having been started. (6) When an ear of popcorn are placed in a microwave oven, the kernels burst into the familiar white, crunchy snack. (7) But they stay attached to the cob, providing individual servings. (8) People enjoys watching the popcorn appear before their eyes. (9) The popcorn-on-the-cob snack has captivated kids whenever it's been available, mainly in the Southwest. (10) The brothers are now experimenting with blue, purple, and red, popcorn cobs. (11) An off-beat option to the traditional varieties, microwave popcorn-on-the-cob is popping up in grocery stores, gift shops, and mail-order catalogs.

20. Sentence 1: **Across the country, popcorn a favorite low-calorie snack.**

What correction should be made to this sentence?

(1) remove the comma after country
(2) insert is after popcorn
(3) insert were after popcorn
(4) add a comma after favorite
(5) no correction is necessary

21. Sentences 2 and 3: **Americans buy over 800 million pounds of unpopped popcorn each year. According to the Popcorn Institute located in Chicago.**

The most effective combination of sentences 2 and 3 would include which of the following groups of words?

(1) in Chicago, Americans buy
(2) year; according
(3) Americans in Chicago
(4) pounds, according
(5) year, however the Popcorn

22. Sentence 4: **Two Brothers from Texas have developed a new variety of popcorn.**

What correction should be made to this sentence?

(1) replace Brothers with brothers
(2) insert a comma after Brothers
(3) replace have with has
(4) insert a comma after variety
(5) no correction is necessary

23. Sentence 5: **Called popcorn-on-the-cob, a new food fad having been started.**

Which of the following is the best way to write the underlined portion of this sentence? If you think the original is the best way, choose option (1).

(1) having been started
(2) have been started
(3) has been started
(4) started to have
(5) were started

24. Sentence 6: **When an ear of popcorn are placed in a microwave oven, the kernels burst into the familiar white, crunchy snack.**

What correction should be made to this sentence?

(1) replace are with is
(2) remove the comma after oven
(3) replace burst with bursted
(4) change the spelling of familiar to famliar
(5) remove the comma after white

25. Sentence 7: **But they stay attached to the cob, providing individual servings.**

Which of the following is the best way to write the underlined portion of this sentence? If you think the original is the best way, choose option (1).

(1) But they stay
(2) Unless they stay
(3) When the kernels stay
(4) The kernels stay
(5) If the kernels stay

26. Sentence 8: **People enjoys watching the popcorn appear before their eyes.**

What correction should be made to this sentence?

(1) replace enjoys with enjoy
(2) insert a comma after popcorn
(3) replace appear with appears
(4) replace their with there
(5) no correction is necessary

27. Sentence 9: **The popcorn-on-the-cob snack has captivated kids whenever it's been available, mainly in the Southwest.**

Which of the following is the best way to write the underlined portion of this sentence? If you think the original is the best way, choose option (1).

(1) has captivated kids whenever
(2) have captivated kids whenever
(3) has captivated kids wherever
(4) have captivated kids wherever
(5) has been captivating kids whenever

28. Sentence 10: **The brothers are now experimenting with blue, purple, and red, popcorn cobs.**

What correction should be made to this sentence?

(1) replace brothers with brothers'
(2) replace are with is
(3) change the spelling of experimenting to experamenting
(4) remove the comma after red
(5) no correction is necessary

29. Sentence 11: **An off-beat option to the traditional varieties, microwave popcorn-on-the-cob is popping up in grocery stores, gift shops, and mail-order catalogs.**

What correction should be made to this sentence?

(1) insert a comma after option
(2) change the spelling of varieties to varietys
(3) replace is with are
(4) replace and with or
(5) no correction is necessary

Items 30–38 refer to the following paragraph.

(1) You're car needs to be washed once a week to remove dirt, city smog, and road salt. (2) Commercial car washes are convienent, but many can harm your car's finish. (3) Unless the car wash uses enough water; the surface of your car can be scratched. (4) Most car washes recycle their water, and if the water isn't properly filtered, salt and dirt could be deposited back on your car. (5) Avoid the car washes that use plastic strip brushes. (6) Those that use cloth pads or rug strips are kinder to your car. (7) The best car washes use high-pressure water, special detergents, and no brushes or pads. (8)The hot wax treatment makes the water bead up on the car's finish, which prevents streaking as the car is driven. (9) The wax only lasts for a week at most. (10) Hand-washing, although it's time-consuming is still the best way to protect your car's finish. (11) An occasional automatic car wash; however, should not be harmful if you pick one that treats your car carefully.

30. Sentence 1: **You're car needs to be washed once a week to remove dirt, city smog, and road salt.**

    What correction should be made to this sentence?

    (1) replace You're with Your
    (2) replace needs with need
    (3) insert a comma after week
    (4) remove the comma after dirt
    (5) replace car with cars'

31. Sentence 2: **Commercial car washes are convienent, but many can harm your car's finish.**

    What correction should be made to this sentence?

    (1) replace are with is
    (2) change the spelling of convienent to convenient
    (3) remove the comma after convienent
    (4) insert a comma after many
    (5) replace car's with cars

32. Sentence 3: **Unless the car wash uses enough water; the surface of your car can be scratched.**

    Which of the following is the best way to write the underlined portion of this sentence? If you think the original is the best way, choose option (1).

    (1) enough water; the
    (2) enough water. The
    (3) enough water, the
    (4) enough water until the
    (5) enough water, and

33. Sentence 4: **Most car washes recycle their water, and if the water isn't properly filtered, salt and dirt could be deposited back on your car.**

    If you rewrote this sentence beginning with

    Since most car washes recycle their water

    the next word should be

    (1) and
    (2) but
    (3) if
    (4) the
    (5) deposits

34. Sentence 6: **Those that use cloth pads or rug strips are kinder to your car.**

    Which of the following is the best way to write the underlined portion of this sentence? If you think the original is the best way, choose option (1).

    (1) Those that use
    (2) Those that uses
    (3) Using those that
    (4) Car washes that use
    (5) Having used car washes

35. Sentence 7: **The best car washes use high-pressure water, special detergents, and no brushes or pads.**

What correction should be made to this sentence?

(1) replace <u>use</u> with <u>uses</u>
(2) remove the comma after <u>water</u>
(3) change the spelling of <u>special</u> to <u>specail</u>
(4) insert a comma after <u>brushes</u>
(5) no correction is necessary

36. Sentences 8 and 9: **The hot wax treatment makes the water bead up on the car's finish, which prevents streaking as the car is driven. The wax only lasts for a week at most.**

The most effective combination of sentences 8 and 9 would include which of the following groups of words?

(1) Since the hot wax
(2) driven, but the
(3) driven, unless the
(4) driven, until the
(5) Because the hot wax

37. Sentence 10: **Hand-washing, although it's time-consuming is still the best way to protect your car's finish.**

What correction should be made to this sentence?

(1) remove the comma after <u>Hand-washing</u>
(2) replace <u>it's</u> with <u>its</u>
(3) insert a comma after <u>time-consuming</u>
(4) replace <u>is</u> with <u>are</u>
(5) no correction is necessary

38. Sentence 11: **An occasional automatic car <u>wash; however, should</u> not be harmful if you pick one that treats your car carefully.**

Which of the following is the best way to write the underlined portion of this sentence? If you think the original is the best way, choose option (1).

(1) wash; however, should
(2) wash; however should
(3) wash, however should
(4) wash, however, should
(5) wash, however; should

Items 39–47 refer to the following paragraph.

(1) Krazy glue, invented in the 1950's, has mend many broken household items. (2) Now the same adhesive found in Krazy glue have been used to close facial cuts and surgical incisions. (3) This "tissue glue" may soon replace stitches, as the best way to mend cuts in the skin without leaving visible scars. (4) Until recently, most plastic surgeons stitched underneath the skin having to avoid scars. (5) Tissue glue can replace stitching completely when and if a cut is small. (6) For larger cuts, tissue glue allow doctors to remove stitches before scar tissue forms around the thread. (7) For closing cuts on a child's face, it is particularly effective. (8) It saves the child from having to return to have stitches removed. (9) It also has reduced the potential of leaving a permanent scar. (10) Physicians, in many cases, are able to lie down their sewing needles and pick up a glue bottle instead.

39. Sentence 1: **Krazy glue, invented in the 1950's, has mend many broken household items.**

   What correction should be made to this sentence?

   (1) remove the comma after glue
   (2) replace has with have
   (3) replace mend with mended
   (4) insert a comma after broken
   (5) no correction is necessary

40. Sentence 2: **Now the same adhesive found in Krazy glue have been used to close facial cuts and surgical incisions.**

   Which of the following is the best way to write the underlined portion of this sentence? If you think the original is the best way, choose option (1).

   (1) glue have been used to
   (2) glue were used to
   (3) glue having been used to
   (4) glue is being used to
   (5) glue being used for to

41. Sentence 3: **This "tissue glue" may soon replace stitches, as the best way to mend cuts in the skin without leaving visible scars.**

   What correction should be made to this sentence?

   (1) remove the comma after stitches
   (2) insert a comma after mend
   (3) replace leaving with to leave
   (4) replace scars with scars'
   (5) no correction is necessary

42. Sentence 4: **Until recently, most plastic surgeons stitched underneath the skin having to avoid scars.**

   Which of the following is the best way to write the underlined portion of this sentence? If you think the original is the best way, choose option (1).

   (1) having to avoid scars
   (2) to avoid scars
   (3) being scars need to be avoided
   (4) having scars avoided
   (5) to have to avoid scars

43. Sentence 5: **Tissue glue can replace stitching completely when and if a cut is small.**

   Which of the following is the best way to write the underlined portion of this sentence? If you think the original is the best way, choose option (1).

   (1) completely when and if a cut
   (2) completely although if a cut
   (3) when and completely a cut
   (4) completely unless a cut
   (5) completely if a cut

44. Sentence 6: **For larger cuts, tissue glue allow doctors to remove stitches before scar tissue forms around the thread.**

What correction should be made to this sentence?

(1) remove the comma after cuts
(2) replace allow with allows
(3) insert a comma after stitches
(4) replace forms with form
(5) no correction is necessary

45. Sentence 7: **For closing cuts on a child's face, it is particularly effective.**

Which of the following is the best way to write the underlined portion of this sentence? If you think the original is the best way, choose option (1).

(1) face, it is
(2) face, it are
(3) face, is tissue glue
(4) face, are tissue glue
(5) face, tissue glue is

46. Sentence 9: **It also has reduced the potential of leaving a permanent scar.**

Which of the following is the best way to write the underlined portion of this sentence? If you think the original is the best way, choose option (1).

(1) also has reduced
(2) also having reduced
(3) also reduces
(4) also have reduced
(5) also had reduced

47. Sentence 10: **Physicians, in many cases, are able to lie down their sewing needles and pick up a glue bottle instead.**

What correction should be made to this sentence?

(1) remove the comma after cases
(2) replace are with is
(3) replace lie with lay
(4) replace their with they're
(5) no correction is necessary

Items 48–55 refer to the following paragraph.

(1) The stress of modern life was taking an immense toll on your health. (2) Current estimates are that 80% of the visits to Doctors in America are for stress-related diseases. (3) While stress itself is hazardous to your health, your reaction to stress affects your body most. (4) When you're under stress, good eating habits are often ignored. (5) You deplete your body of essential nutrients. (6) Stress also makes your body secrete additional hormones which speed up their bodily functions. (7) Scientist's are convinced that relaxation is the key to coping with stress. (8) When you're relaxed, your heart and rate of breathing slow down. (9) Tense muscles ease and blood pressure declines. (10) By learning how to relax for just ten minutes a day, you can lower your stress level and more energy can be had. (11) You can control your stress instead of allowing your stress to control you.

48. Sentence 1: **The stress of modern life was taking an immense toll on your health.**

    Which of the following is the best way to write the underlined portion of this sentence? If you think the original is the best way, choose option (1).

    (1) life was taking
    (2) life have been taking
    (3) life may be taking
    (4) life were taking
    (5) life has been taking

49. Sentence 2: **Current estimates are that 80% of the visits to Doctors in America are for stress-related diseases.**

    What correction should be made to this sentence?

    (1) insert a comma after are
    (2) insert a comma after visits
    (3) replace Doctors with doctors
    (4) replace for with because
    (5) change the spelling of diseases to disaeses

50. Sentence 3: **While stress itself is hazardous to your health, your reaction to stress affects your body most.**

    What correction should be made to this sentence?

    (1) replace While with Until
    (2) replace is with are
    (3) remove the comma after health
    (4) replace affects with effects
    (5) replace most with more

51. Sentences 4 and 5: **When you're under stress, good eating habits are often ignored. You deplete your body of essential nutrients.**

    The most effective combination of sentences 4 and 5 would include which of the following groups of words?

    (1) stress habits are
    (2) ignored, thereby depleting
    (3) essential nutrients that
    (4) ignored, but you
    (5) your body under stress

52. Sentence 6: **Stress also makes your body secrete additional hormones which speed up their bodily functions.**

What correction should be made to this sentence?

(1) replace makes with make
(2) change the spelling of additional to additonal
(3) replace speed with speeds
(4) replace their with your
(5) no correction is necessary

53. Sentence 7: **Scientist's are convinced that relaxation is the key to coping with stress.**

What correction should be made to this sentence?

(1) replace Scientist's with Scientists
(2) replace are with has been
(3) replace is with are
(4) insert a comma after key
(5) no correction is necessary

54. Sentence 8: **When you're relaxed, your heart and rate of breathing slow down.**

Which of the following is the best way to write the underlined portion of this sentence? If you think the original is the best way, choose option (1).

(1) and rate of breathing
(2) and breathing rates
(3) and to breathe more slowly
(4) and breathing more slowly
(5) and slow breathing rate

55. Sentence 10: **By learning how to relax for just ten minutes a day, you can lower your stress level and more energy can be had.**

Which of the following is the best way to write the underlined portion of this sentence? If you think the original is the best way, choose option (1).

(1) more energy can be had
(2) having more energy
(3) to have more energy
(4) feel more energetic
(5) feeling more energy

Answers are on page 104.

WRITING SKILLS, PART II
Directions

Part II of the Writing Skills Test determines how well you write. You will have 45 minutes to write an essay that explains or presents an opinion or states a view on an issue. Follow these steps:

1. Carefully read the directions and the essay topic below.

2. Plan your essay before you write. Stick to the topic.

3. Use scratch paper to make notes.

4. Write your essay on a copy of the answer sheet on page 110. Write legibly and use a ballpoint pen so that your evaluator will be able to read your writing.

5. Read what you have written, and make any changes that will improve your essay.

6. Check your essay for sentence structure, spelling, punctuation, capitalization, and usage. Make any necessary corrections.

Topic

In many families with young children, the parents work outside the home. Many of these parents take their children to day-care centers during work hours. In other families with young children, one parent stays at home to care for the children.

Write a composition of about 200 words in which you compare and contrast the experience of children whose parents care for them at home with the experience of children who are cared for at day-care centers during work hours. Be specific and cite examples to support your comparison.

Model answer and correction instructions are on pages 106 and 108.

Adapted with permission of the American Council on Education.

☰ Analysis of Performance: Writing Skills Simulated Test B

Name: _____ Class: _____ Date: _____

Part I

The chart below will help you determine your strengths and weaknesses in grammar usage, sentence structure, and mechanics (spelling, capitalization, and punctuation).

Directions

Circle the number of each item that you answered correctly on the Simulated GED Test B. Count the number of items you answered correctly in each column. Write the amount in the <u>Total Correct</u> space of each column. (For example, if you answered 13 Mechanics items correctly, place the number 13 in the blank before <u>out of 13</u>). Complete this process for the remaining columns.

Count the number of items you answered correctly in each row. Write that amount in the <u>Total Correct</u> space of each row. (For example, in the <u>Construction Shift</u> row, write the number correct in the blank before <u>out of 7</u>). Complete this process for the remaining rows.

Test B Analysis of Performance Chart

Item Types:	Mechanics (Unit 1)	Usage (Unit 2)	Sentence Structure (Unit 3)	Total Correct
Construction Shift		7	4, 13, 21, 33, 36, 51	_____ out of 7
Sentence Correction	1, 16, 19, 22, 28, 31, 37, 41, 49, 53	5, 8, 9, 14, 24, 26, 30, 39, 44, 50, 52	2, 11, 20, 29, 35, 47	_____ out of 27
Sentence Revision	3, 32, 38	10, 15, 17, 23, 25, 34, 40, 45, 46, 48	6, 12, 18, 27, 42, 43, 54, 55	_____ out of 21
Total Correct	_____ out of 13	_____ out of 22	_____ out of 20	Total Correct: _____ out of 55 1–40 = You need more review 41–55 = Congratulations! You're ready

If you answered fewer than 41 of the 55 items correctly, determine which areas are hardest for you. Go back to the *Steck-Vaughn GED Writing Skills* book and review the content in those specific areas.

In the parentheses under the heading, the unit numbers tell you where you can find the beginning of specific instruction about that area of grammar in the *Steck-Vaughn GED Writing Skills* book. Also refer to the chart on page 3.

Part II

Have your instructor or another person read and score your essay. Essays are scored on a scale of * to 6, with * the lowest score and 6 the highest score. Follow the instructions on page 108.

Enter the reader's score here _____

Ask the reader to help you determine the strong points of the essay and areas where the essay needs improvement. The feedback you receive from the reader will help you improve the next essay you write.

Answers and Explanations

UNIT 1: MECHANICS

Capitalization
Page 4

The corrected words are:
1. director, state
2. South
3. Doctor
4. Japanese, German
5. correct as written
6. Pollution
7. federal government, war
8. Pacific Ocean
9. Jamaica, tourist
10. high school, Community College
11. correct as written
12. world, Africa
13. spring, unions
14. French, Italian
15. There, city, utility

Comma Use I
Page 5

1. Volunteers to prepare food, package individual meals, and deliver food to elderly shut-ins are needed by the Community Action Center.

2. Answering questions regarding nuclear waste, the spokesperson for the electric company was visibly nervous.

3. Anthony Ching, the union's shop steward, provides the company with a list of repairs needed each week to ensure worker safety.

4. The newspaper editor asked the reporter to investigate the accident, determine the real cause, and identify the person responsible for the damage.

5. Until she had completed the probationary period, the new employee was not allowed to use the chemicals alone.

6. To fully understand the situation, the dismayed parents asked to speak to the principal.

7. Patients are taught about sound nutrition, appropriate exercise, and stress reduction.

8. Mrs. Landover, the most active club member, suggested conducting a bowl-a-thon to raise money.

9. After the job was completed, the contractor checked to see if the customers were satisfied.

10. Pittsburgh, Pennsylvania, is located where the Allegheny and Monongahela rivers come together to form the Ohio River.

11. The list containing the names, addresses, and phone numbers of each of the applicants was given to the employment office.

12. Jonathan Welch, a senator from Texas, introduced legislation that would provide stricter punishment for drug pushers.

13. On the way to her job, Ms. Chaney drops off her daughter at the Sunshine Child Care Center.

14. Isaac Asimov, an award winning scientist, also wrote many books.

15. When spring begins, many Americans prepare their income tax forms for the Internal Revenue Service.

16. Our summer garden is producing corn, squash, tomatoes, cucumbers, and green peppers.

17. Wind, insects, bats, birds, moths, and butterflies help plants to transfer their pollen from the male to the female plants.

18. Agates, semiprecious stones, have bands of different colors.

19. Table salt, a mineral, is found in rocks, soil, and oceans.

20. The sentence is correct as written.

21. Swimming, jogging, walking, and riding bicycles are all good forms of exercise.

Comma Use II
Page 6

The correctly punctuated sentences are:
1. The vocational component of Dawson Technical Institute offers programs in machine repair, data processing, and respiratory therapy.

2. The woman who identified the criminal was given a reward by the prosecutors.

3. The carpet, which they purchased only two years ago, was completely ruined by the flood.

4. To comply with state health regulations, people without shoes are not allowed into most restaurants.

5. The sentence is correct as written.

6. The anxious father paced the floor and talked continuously until his wife delivered the baby.

7. Mr. McArthur, a self-made millionaire, is a major contributor to the minority scholarship program.

8. Yesterday the excited bride-to-be bought the invitations, addressed the envelopes, and deposited them in the mail.

9. Because of the delay in processing the orders, the managers asked the employees to work overtime.

10. The driver of the car that went speeding through the red light was stopped immediately by the police.

11. Victor, recommended by his supervisor, was given a promotion to line foreman.

12. Sarah Williams, whom I've known for fifteen years, was given the Outstanding Adult Student Award for her commitment to helping others further their education.

13. The sentence is correct as written.

14. Wanting to lose weight in order to improve his health, Mr. Ferro contacted several diet programs.

15. When planting flowers or vegetables, always water the ground thoroughly.

16. The sentence is correct as written.

17. The car with the sun roof, power windows, and power locks is the one I want.

18. The sentence is correct as written.

19. Rollerblading, also called inline skating, became a popular sport during the 1990s.

20. Knowing how to use a computer has become an important job skill.

21. Anna's friends took her to lunch and gave her a cake for her birthday.

22. During their vacation, the Monroes plan to repaint their house, plant a garden, and clean out the garage.

23. The man at the next table is talking so loudly that we cannot carry on our own conversation.

24. Benjamin's aunt, uncle, and cousin came to visit him during the holidays.

Semicolons and Commas
Page 7
The correctly punctuated sentences are:

1. Mrs. Sheared works full-time, but she also attends Washington Evening School to prepare for her GED examination.

2. According to management, the painters are paid an adequate salary; however, the painters are continuing to request salary raises.

3. The caseworkers were upset; they had just been informed that the child had run away from home again.

4. Many people believe that drunk drivers should have their licenses revoked; moreover, they believe that drunk drivers who are involved in accidents should go to jail.

5. Doctors urge patients to develop a healthier diet, and they encourage regular exercise to strengthen the heart muscle.

6. The number of African American, Hispanic, and Asian minorities is growing; in fact, by the year 2010, almost 40 percent of the population under 18 will be minority.

7. The unpopular candidate tried to address the key issues in the campaign, but the angry crowd kept interrupting his speech.

8. Discrimination based on gender has been made illegal; however, many women proclaim that it still exists.

9. The phone customers were enraged; the long distance call rate was being increased again.

10. Only 15 percent of court-ordered child support is ever paid by fathers; consequently, many children are not receiving adequate support.

11. Let's stop at that new restaurant; I'm starving.

12. The Andersons must leave at 6:00 A.M.; otherwise, they will miss their flight to Los Angeles.

13. The American Heart Association urges middle-aged men to get cholesterol screenings, and they suggest a low-fat diet to lower a high cholesterol level.

14. Marilyn can return to school next semester, or she can look for a job.

15. His hobby is gardening; her hobby is playing the piano.

Apostrophes
Page 8
The words that need apostrophes are:

1.	buyer's	15.	reporter's
2.	suspect's	16.	family's, wasn't
3.	Florida's	17.	isn't
4.	missiles' fuel tanks	18.	We're, neighbors'
5.	drivers'	19.	company's
6.	correct as written	20.	didn't, I'll
7.	couldn't, children's	21.	he'd, didn't, I've
8.	weren't	22.	plan's
9.	car's, hadn't	23.	Hasn't
10.	correct as written	24.	sons'
11.	it's	25.	You're
12.	Frank's, won't	26.	don't
13.	President's	27.	City's
14.	Chicago's	28.	correct as written

Quotation Marks
Page 9

1. The mayor's aide reported, "Mayor Stillwater has appointed an interim director to fill the vacancy caused by Ms. Terrell's resignation."

2. The hotel manager announced, "There will be a complimentary dinner for those guests who were disturbed by the noise."

3. The lottery winner screamed, "I can't believe I won!"

4. "Although you can't say that stress directly causes people to be ill," said the health counselor, "stress does significantly affect a person's general health."

5. "When the tenants band together to protest unsanitary living conditions, the landlords are more easily persuaded to make improvements," explained the lawyer.

6. At an international meeting to support a ban on ozone-destroying chemicals, the concerned representative noted, "The Earth's ozone helps filter the sun's ultraviolet rays that cause skin cancer. Without it, we would all die."

7. Speaking about a proposed law to ban pornography, the activist said, "We are drowning in garbage, and this law is a long overdue lifeline."

8. An unemployment specialist reported, "Low pay is the top reason that millions of one-worker households are poor."

9. "Eat plenty of fruit and vegetables," said the dietician, "if you want to be sure you have enough vitamins in your diet."

10. "You'll always be welcome here," whispered Leon's brother, "and you don't need an invitation."

11. "We provide the best service," claimed the car dealer, "and can arrange financing for almost anyone."

12. Former Detroit mayor Coleman Young once told reporters, "One thing you learn as mayor is how long it takes to get something done; you have to stay on it."

13. When asked how soon Americans will have smart credit cards, the expert advised, "Not right away; it's expensive to put the computer terminals in stores that accept the cards."

14. "If you wouldn't give your baby a bottle of gin the day after birth, why give it one the day before?" asked the doctor who advised pregnant mothers against drinking alcohol.

15. "Inpatient mental hospitalization of teenagers has increased dramatically," said the doctor to the audience of concerned parents.

16. "Whether Pete Rose gambles on the baseball field is his own business," said my brother, but I replied, "No, because he's a public figure that kids look up to, it's everyone's business."

17. "Research has shown," said the biologist, "that Britain's five million house cats kill over twenty million birds a year."

18. Explaining why customers received monthly bills exceeding $10,000, the company spokesperson said, "The computer had a malfunction in the program that prepares the bills."

Spelling Practice I
Page 14

1. site
2. whether
3. personnel
4. c
5. role
6. great
7. brakes
8. accepted
9. principal's
10. c
11. week
12. pair
13. scene
14. peace
15. c
16. knew
17. meat
18. There

Spelling Practice II
Page 15

1. dessert
2. opportunity
3. governor's
4. fundamental
5. piece
6. permanent
7. correct
8. muscle
9. practical
10. correct
11. business
12. approval
13. development
14. receive

GED Practice: Mechanics
Pages 16–19

1. **(2) change the spelling of ocassional to occasional** Occasional is the correct spelling. The pronoun everyone does not need to be capitalized. The semicolon is necessary to separate two independent clauses. No commas are needed.

2. **(2) insert a comma after psychological** An interrupting phrase must have commas before and after it. The comma after insomnia is also needed for that reason. No other commas are needed.

3. **(4) include pain, use of** Use a comma to separate items in a list. No other choice has the correct punctuation.

4. **(1) change the spelling of recomend to recommend** Recommend is the correct spelling. No commas are needed.

5. **(2) exercising vigorously, avoiding** Use a comma to separate items in a list. No other choice has the correct punctuation.

6. **(1) change the spelling of specailist to specialist** Specialist is the correct spelling. No internal punctuation is needed in this sentence.

7. **(5) no correction is necessary.**

8. **(3) sleep by not allowing** No internal punctuation is needed in this sentence.

9. **(1) change the spelling of differant to different** Different is the correct spelling. There is no reason to capitalize everyone. No commas are needed.

10. **(3) remove the comma after cured** There is no reason to use a comma after cured. The comma, not a semicolon, after bothersome is necessary to separate two independent clauses joined by but.

11. **(2) insert a comma after trees** A comma is needed to set off the interrupting phrase. The comma after earth is needed for the same reason. The possessive form of California is needed to show ownership of the trees. No other commas are needed.

12. **(2) replace sprouts' with sprouts** Sprouts is used as a plural predicate noun and thus the possessive form is not needed. No commas are needed. Vikings must be capitalized because it is a proper noun.

13. **(4) replace Million with million** A common noun should not be capitalized. No commas are needed. Redwoods is the subject of the sentence, not a possessive noun.

14. **(3) replace west with West** West must be capitalized since it refers to a section of the country. No internal punctuation is needed.

15. **(5) no correction is necessary.**

16. **(3) remove the comma after mosses** Do not use a comma to separate two objects connected by the word and. No commas are needed in this sentence.

17. **(1) replace park with Park** Park is a part of a title and therefore must be capitalized. Northern does not need to be capitalized because it refers to a direction, not an area of the country. The comma after California is needed to set off the interrupting phrase.

18. **(2) by bus, but** Two independent clauses joined with a connecting word must have a comma before the conjunction. No other punctuation is needed.

19. **(1) replace parks with park's.** The possessive form is needed to show ownership of the terrain. Park does not need to be capitalized because it is not a proper noun. No commas are needed.

20. **(3) remove the comma after <u>year</u>** No internal punctuation is needed in this sentence.

21. **(1) replace <u>particuler</u> with <u>particular</u>** Particular is the correct spelling. Both commas are needed to set off the interrupting phrase. No other punctuation is needed.

22. **(3) remove the quotation marks** These words are not a direct quotation of someone's words, so quotation marks are not needed. All spelling is correct. The comma is needed to set off an interrupting phrase.

23. **(2) redwoods and preserve** The only punctuation needed in this sentence is the comma that separates the introductory phrase from the rest of the sentence.

UNIT 2: USAGE

Subject/Verb Agreement I
Page 20

1.	has	11.	expect
2.	were	12.	dump
3.	has	13.	is
4.	increases	14.	plan
5.	try	15.	become
6.	has	16.	is
7.	want	17.	avoid
8.	Does	18.	eat
9.	take	19.	are
10.	brings	20.	float

Subject/Verb Agreement II
Page 21

1.	anticipate	12.	expects
2.	was	13.	has
3.	believe	14.	want
4.	agree	15.	contain
5.	were	16.	has
6.	was	17.	are
7.	have, need	18.	encourage
8.	have	19.	are
9.	has	20.	need
10.	were, were	21.	has
11.	was or were	22.	wants

Subject/Verb Agreement III
Page 22

1.	was	9.	checks
2.	C	10.	show
3.	were	11.	has
4.	C	12.	C
5.	relates	13.	say
6.	are	14.	were
7.	C	15.	were
8.	Does		

Irregular Verbs I
Page 23

1.	forgiven	10.	blew
2.	written	11.	known
3.	done	12.	sang
4.	took	13.	forbidden
5.	given	14.	fallen
6.	begun	15.	done
7.	hurt	16.	felt
8.	spoke	17.	heard
9.	rung		

Irregular Verbs II
Page 24

1.	swam	9.	shaken
2.	sprayed	10.	forgotten
3.	driven	11.	sang
4.	frozen	12.	given
5.	broken	13.	spoke
6.	bled	14.	taken
7.	drawn	15.	eaten
8.	gone	16.	washed

Verb Tenses
Page 25

1.	decreased	8.	ignored
2.	reports	9.	increased
3.	will purchase	10.	sponsors
4.	remains	11.	refused
5.	sent	12.	is requesting
6.	will have	13.	is planting
7.	warn	14.	is rising

Perfect Tense
Page 26

1.	has increased	9.	had begun
2.	will have declined	10.	had had
3.	had learned	11.	has offered
4.	had understood	12.	will have planted
5.	will have visited	13.	have eaten
6.	had notified	14.	will decide
7.	had inspected	15.	will have worked
8.	suggested	16.	has approved

Commonly Confused Verbs
Page 27

1.	raising	9.	lying
2.	lying	10.	sitting
3.	set	11.	risen
4.	rise	12.	rising
5.	set	13.	lay
6.	laid	14.	risen
7.	setting	15.	laid
8.	lain	16.	sat

17. rose	20. raised
18. sat	21. set
19. lay	22. sit

GED Practice: Verbs
Pages 28–29

1. **(3) replace uses with use** The plural verb use matches its subject <u>farmers</u>. <u>Contain</u> matches its implied subject <u>fruits</u> and <u>vegetables</u>. No commas are needed.

2. **(4) replace improves with improve** Both verbs (preserve and <u>improve</u>) must be plural to match the subject <u>Some of these chemicals</u>. No commas are needed.

3. **(4) replace caused with cause** The rest of the passage is in the present tense and <u>cause</u> is a present tense verb. No comma is needed.

4. **(1) you can take** The sentence is correct as written.

5. **(2) replace are with is** The singular verb is matches the gerund subject <u>washing</u>. The verb <u>wash</u> cannot be used as a subject. No commas are needed.

6. **(5) no correction is necessary**

7. **(4) replace needs with need** The plural <u>need</u> matches the subject <u>foods</u>, as does the verb <u>have</u>. The comma after <u>foods</u> sets off an interrupting clause.

8. **(2) that contains** Only option (2) contains a singular verb in the present tense.

9. **(2) insert a comma after leaves** A comma is needed to separate two independent clauses joined by a conjunction.

10. **(4) that you have grown** The past participle form of a verb must be used when a helping word is present. The correct past participle of <u>grow</u> is <u>grown</u>. The other choices do not make sense.

11. **(4) replace was with were** The plural verb were matches its subject. The other verbs in the sentence are correct in tense and form. No comma is needed.

12. **(4) replace will have been with has been** Has been is the helping verb needed with <u>grown</u> to reflect the appropriate time meaning of the sentence. The comma after <u>However</u> sets off an introductory word. The verb <u>can buy</u> is used correctly. No additional commas are needed in the sentence.

Plural and Possessive Nouns
Page 30

1. problems	8. agencies
2. rights	9. people
3. government's	10. communities
4. opinions	11. stores'
5. businesses	12. shelves
6. deer's or deers'	13. crash's
7. eye's	14. children's

Personal Pronouns
Page 31

1. his, him	3. he
2. them	4. us

5. we	11. your
6. hers, she	12. theirs
7. its	13. them
8. you, your	14. we
9. me, mine	15. you, I
10. them, our	16. your, them

Pronoun Antecedents
Page 32

1.	his	Mr. Peabody
2.	its	cat
3.	their	Baileys, they
4.	its	house
5.	their	Edward, Allan
6.	her	Ms. Gutierrez
7.	its	box
8.	her	Jennifer, Maxine
9.	it	duffel bag
10.	his	Jimmy, Sam
11.	their	The people
12.	her	Mother Nature
13.	their	Americans
14.	its	computer program
15.	their	parents

Indefinite Pronoun Antecedents
Page 33

1. his		13. his
2. his		14. her
3. his		15. his
4. themselves		16. their
5. his		17. his or her
6. his		18. her
7. her		19. his
8. their		20. they
9. his		21. she
10. its		22. its
11. they		23. she
12. his		24. his or her

Pronoun Errors
Page 34

1. Terry, Jose, and he took their wives out to dinner together.

2. Tonight the Browns and we are going to see the just-released movie.

3. The general did not know it was they who arrived at the military base.

4. The reporter asked if it was I who reported the fire.

5. While playing at the park, the children and he found a stray cat that they brought home.

6. After the wedding, Mr. and Mrs. Santucci and they stopped by the house before going to the reception.

7. Gina and I would like to take courses to improve our computer skills.

Who/Whom
Page 35

1.	whom	14.	who
2.	who	15.	Whoever
3.	whom	16.	whom
4.	whomever	17.	who, who
5.	who	18.	who
6.	who	19.	whom
7.	whom	20.	who
8.	who	21.	who
9.	whomever	22.	whomever
10.	whom	23.	who
11.	who	24.	who
12.	who	25.	whom
13.	Whoever	26.	Whom

Homonyms
Page 36

1.	its	10.	You're
2.	who's	11.	it's
3.	It's	12.	your
4.	they're	13.	who's
5.	there	14.	their
6.	whose	15.	they're
7.	your	16.	there
8.	their	17.	whose
9.	its	18.	they're

Adjectives
Page 37

1.	better	9.	neater
2.	most patient	10.	more comfortable
3.	less expensive	11.	most dangerous
4.	the biggest lobster	12.	more rested
5.	more difficult	13.	quieter
6.	smoother	14.	funniest
7.	most unusual	15.	angrier
8.	faster	16.	older

GED Practice: Usage
Pages 38–41

1. **(2) replace are with is** The singular verb is is needed to match the subject symbol.

2. **(5) no correction is necessary** The sentence is correct as written.

3. **(5) no correction is necessary**

4. **(3) insert a comma after peaches** The comma is needed to separate items in a series.

5. **(4) as well; for example,** The conjunction for example joins two independent clauses. It needs a semicolon before it, and a comma after it.

6. **(3) replace does with do** The plural verb do is needed to match the subject they. The comma is needed to separate two independent clauses.

7. **(2) are beginning to offer** The rest of the passage is in the present tense. Only option (2) is in present tense and matches the plural subject.

8. **(4) replace whom with who** Who serves as the subject of the phrase who otherwise would go elsewhere.

9. **(2) not only offer food** The plural verb offer is needed to match the subject supermarkets.

10. **(4) remove more** Do not use the word more or most in a simple description that is not a comparison.

11. **(4) replace has with have** The plural verb have is needed to match its subject Americans.

12. **(1) replace they're with their** The possessive pronoun their is needed to show ownership.

13. **(2) than there had been** Only option (2) makes sense for tense agreement in this sentence.

14. **(5) replace shares with share** The plural verb share matches the subject people.

15. **(2) replace parents' with parents** The possessive form is not needed as the noun is used as the object of a preposition.

16. **(3) replace keeps with keep** The plural verb keep is needed to match its subject services.

17. **(5) no correction is necessary** The sentence is correct as written.

18. **(4) replace them with elderly people** Elderly people is needed to clarify who keeps active.

19. **(2) replace Their with There** The adverb There is needed, not the possessive pronoun.

20. **(2) isn't able to cook** Only option (2) has a singular, present tense verb.

21. **(1) replace are with is** Either is always singular and requires a singular verb is.

22. **(4) change the spelling of temperment to temperament** Temperament is the correct spelling.

23. **(1) replace them with they** They is the correct pronoun form as part of the compound subject.

UNIT 3: SENTENCE STRUCTURE

Sentence Fragments
Page 42

Sentences will vary with students. Following are examples of correct sentences.

1. A class of adults is learning about how to make their own car repairs.

2. S

3. The laborers' union council will meet to decide what sites to picket.

4. The person was charged with drunken driving after falling asleep at a traffic light.

5. Mr. Contreras, the only resident who is against the plan, did not attend.

6. She plans to buy the deluxe vacuum cleaner since it is on sale.

7. S

8. A survey of twenty-two cities that are considering new property taxes was conducted.

9. S

10. A contract was issued to repair over half of the state's crumbling bridges.

11. After deciding on going to the lake and buying the necessary fishing permits, we began our trip.

12. The low-income housing project will be located near Huntley Park.

13. S

14. S

15. Educators plan to boycott the reduction of funds for the community college library's computer system.

16. S

17. Most of the drug-related deaths reported in 1995 were caused by cocaine.

18. On the way to the local discount store, I saw a video store's offer of three movies for $5.00.

19. S

20. The school committee member argued that "children have the right to know how to protect themselves."

21. S

22. When the polls have closed and all the votes have finally been counted, the candidate will know if she is the new state senator.

Run-On Sentences
Page 43
Sample paragraphs follow. They could be corrected in other ways.

Paragraph 1:

   People who have been divorced know that the breakup of a marriage can leave deep scars on their children. Children often think they are at fault for the divorce. They blame themselves for being "bad" children. Children are also afraid that they will become latchkey kids. Sometimes they fear that they will become homeless or have to live in a shelter. They may have fantasies about the absent parent returning. Some become victims of custody battles and have to choose between their mother and father.

Paragraph 2:

   The credit card industry is less than forty years old. Some credit cards have offered real convenience. Those accepting credit cards include hospitals for open-heart surgery and the federal government for income taxes. Credit cards have made debt the American way of life. Instead of saving for a washer and dryer, some people merely charge them. They do not realize that it may cost them more to charge than to pay cash. As a result of easy access to credit, many American families are over their heads in debt.

Sentence Combining I
Page 44
Answers may vary. Following are examples.

1. ; however,
2. , but
3. , or
4. ; consequently,
5. ; otherwise,
6. ; in addition,
7. ; for example,
8. , and

9. , but
10. ; meanwhile,
11. , nor
12. , but
13. ; therefore,
14. ; otherwise,
15. ; for example,
16. ; however,
17. ; for example,

Sentence Combining II
Page 45
Sentences will vary. Following are some examples.

1. Advanced Business System's training program was very costly, but their record of job placement was excellent.

2. Although she often gets tired of the paperwork, the police officer is very efficient.

3. Last week he bought on sale a new set of carpet mats for the car.

4. Most brands of lunch meat contain artificial preservatives that are used to retard spoilage.

5. We can leave for the restaurant as soon as I make these phone calls.

6. While I finish washing the windows, could you please mow the lawn?

7. Some companies use drug testing as a standard part of their pre-employment process.

8. Even though grocery stores in the inner city and the suburbs are often run by the same company, there are often differences in prices for the same product.

9. "Happy Days Are Here Again" was one of the most well-known, popular songs of the 1930's.

10. The package, addressed to her grandchild, was mailed on Wednesday by Mrs. Sinata.

11. The report, recently filed by the Internal Investigation Unit, caused controversy within the agency.

12. The list showed that fees vary widely; for example, lawyers charged from $225 to $2,500 for an uncontested divorce.

13. The Disney-MGM Studios Theme Park, near Orlando, Florida, cost $500 million to build.

14. General Motors' Corvette ZR1 has a top speed of 180 m.p.h. and can go from 0 to 60 m.p.h. in 4.2 seconds.

15. Although scientists R. Stanley Pons and Martin Fleischmann claimed they found a simpler way to generate fusion, many other scientists said that their work was flawed.

16. Because I had a car accident when I was sixteen, I had nightmares for ten years afterward.

17. Child safety seats have become important devices because they reduce injury to children in car accidents.

18. It will stop raining soon; then we can go for a walk or to the park.

19. A VCR allows viewers to tape TV shows to be watched at a more convenient time.

Parallel Structure
Page 46
1. The residents volunteered to board up abandoned buildings, wash graffiti off the walls, and patrol the park.

2. The employees were asked to stock the shelves, take inventory, and sweep the floor.

3. Beginning the preparations now will be better than postponing them.

4. To prevent crime, both police protection and community involvement are necessary.

5. Mr. Cutter thinks travel is exciting because it allows him an opportunity to meet new people and to see different places.

6. The hospital staff asked the patient for his name, address, and phone number.

7. People tend to exercise more regularly if they take part in more than one activity; for example, a person could alternate bicycling, walking, and swimming occasionally.

8. It's quiet now because Josh is sleeping, Trina is playing outside, and Brian is reading a book.

9. On the weekends we enjoy going out to eat, shopping in the malls, and driving in the country.

10. Many fast food restaurants' milkshakes are not made with milk but with fillers, flavorings, and added chemicals.

11. When examining a house, always check for water marks on the walls, water pressure in the faucets, and sediment in the pipes.

12. A small family business has a better chance of being profitable if its product is unique, uses common ingredients, and has fairly low prices.

13. To live well requires a belief in one's self, an attitude of fairness, and a desire to help others.

14. Using fertilizer, watering regularly, and weeding every week can improve the harvest from your garden.

15. The Bill of Rights guarantees our freedom of speech, our right to assemble peacefully, and our right to bear arms.

16. Neither exercising nor eating less food is the best way to lose weight; the best way is to combine the two.

17. Reading good books, watching movies, and playing softball are three of my favorite hobbies.

18. At noon I'll deposit my paycheck, put gas in the car, and buy some bread.

19. Painting pictures and playing music are two ways for individuals to express their creativity.

20. The special dinner at China Palace comes with egg rolls, fried rice, and wonton soup.

Subordination I
Page 47
Sentences will vary. Some examples follow.

1. Johnson has to leave early in order to pick up his son from the day care center.

2. Since the hurricane had destroyed the mobile home park, the federal government provided emergency assistance.

3. Newspapers can give specific details of a story, whereas television news usually only reports the general outline.

4. Because toothpastes now contain fluoride, tooth decay has decreased significantly.

5. Because the quality of future life depends on us, the Environmental Protection Agency wants to act now to protect the environment.

6. Even if we could save enough money for the down payment, we would still need to have money for moving costs and initial repairs.

7. When I take Mother to visit her friends, I will stop at the cleaners and drop off the clothes.

8. The new findings show that dairy products contain fat as well as calcium and vitamins.

9. Although I would like to go with you, I have to care for my sister's children since she's in the hospital.

10. Unless the problem of drugs is addressed, many of our children will become victims.

11. Since I don't get home from work until after 6:00, I miss seeing the 5:30 TV news shows every day.

12. Because my dental hygienist is gentle and does not cause me discomfort when she cleans my teeth, I plan to continue getting my teeth cleaned every six months.

13. After I save money from my paycheck this month, I will be able to buy a new CD player.

14. The band has been playing much better recently because they have been practicing a lot and learning new material.

Subordination II
Page 48

1. b	5. b	9. b	13. b
2. a	6. b	10. b	14. a
3. a	7. a	11. a	15. a
4. a	8. b	12. a	16. a

Sentence Revising I
Page 49
1. Because the mayor was under pressure, he had to act quickly.

2. Bubba went to the Department of Public Safety office in order to take the driver's license examination.

3. The woman who provided the information which led to the conviction was given the reward money.

4. We didn't have any hot water because the electricity that runs the water heater has been off since the storm.

5. If I take enough time to assemble the ingredients, the recipe will be easy to prepare.

Sentence Revising II
Page 50
1. While swimming has traditionally been a popular recreational activity, concern about safety keeps thousands of swimmers off the beaches.

2. Because portable telephones can be used for business, home, and leisure, they are becoming widely popular.

3. The largest amusement park in America, Cedar Point, is located in Sandusky, Ohio.

UNIT 3

4. If fifteen lifeguards are not hired by May 30, Little Rock won't be able to open its municipal pools.

5. The fire marshal reported that an increase in destructive fatal fires in Idaho shows the public indifference to safety.

6. Since the drummer in the rock band has taken a regular job, he won't be available.

Sentence Revising III
Page 51
1. a   3. b   5. a   7. a
2. b   4. b   6. a

GED Practice: Sentence Revising I
Page 52
1. 4   3. 1   5. 4
2. 3   4. 5   6. 3

GED Practice: Sentence Revising II
Page 53
1. 3   3. 3   5. 2
2. 2   4. 1   6. 2

Misplaced Modifiers
Page 54
Some sentences can be corrected in more than one way. Following are examples of corrected sentences.

1. My neighbor bought the used car with low mileage from a reputable dealer.

2. The plant supervisor discussed during lunch the possibility of implementing the employee medical coverage plan.

3. In the boss's office, we discussed plans for the annual company picnic.

4. I returned the defective lawn mower that I had bought to the store.

5. The chef's assistant mixed the ingredients for the cake filling in the blender.

6. The janitor located the missing file behind the secretary's desk.

7. Mr. Meyers yelled angrily at the children who were playing in the street.

8. The sentence is correct as written.

9. The caseworker with the beautiful long hair was explaining the application procedure to a client in the lobby.

10. Jorge looked sadly at the newly purchased car, destroyed by the fallen tree.

11. Mrs. Cheng found the missing lottery tickets jammed under the doorway.

12. We waved to the smiling boy coming up the driveway on a skateboard.

13. Jennifer was cleaning out the file cabinet containing over fifty-four software disks.

14. The painter, wearing overalls, began work on the rented house.

15. The Mississippi River, which is over two miles wide, has been polluted by factory waste.

16. We couldn't locate the keys, covered by papers on the desk, to the computer room.

17. Mrs. Kaspar was waiting impatiently for her physician to call with the test results.

18. The sentence is correct as written.

19. The police officers caught the bank manager, who had been embezzling funds for years, disposing of the incriminating evidence.

20. Elwin purchased a compact disc player with seven special features from the audio store.

21. Manufacturers are trying to produce a cigarette made of herbs for smokers.

22. Before Richard left to play golf all afternoon, he fed the cat.

23. Have you ever been bitten by fire ants when you were working in the garden?

24. Coming up on your left is the American Mutual Life building.

Dangling Modifiers
Page 55
Sentences may vary. Following are some example sentences.

1. While I was enjoying lunch with my co-workers, my car was stolen.

2. While the ambulance was being driven to the hospital, it was hit by another car.

3. The sentence is correct as written.

4. When I was thirteen, my family moved back East.

5. While I was walking home from the bus stop, my umbrella was caught by the wind and blew away.

6. The sentence is correct as written.

7. While I was waiting for the check to arrive in the mail, the bills became overdue.

8. After I had worked all day, the bed was a welcome sight.

9. While I was rushing to get to work, the flat tire on the car caused a delay.

10. The sentence is correct as written.

11. When I was parking at the mall, my car was hit by a man who wasn't paying attention to what he was doing.

12. As they were wondering what to do next, the assembly line stopped while the supervisors discussed the problem.

13. I was exhausted and sunburned, so my trip soon came to an end.

14. The sentence is correct as written.

15. As we were walking through the discount store, we saw that the aisles were cluttered with merchandise.

16. The real estate agent showed us the big house that was old and worn out.

17. After I read the recipe, I baked a casserole for the guests.

18. While I was speaking to a group of strangers, my knees knocked and my hands shook.

UNIT 3

19. Before he booked the thief, the police officer advised the thief of his right to consult a lawyer.

20. While I was walking in the park, a huge dog bit my leg.

21. While Pat was reeling in the line quickly, the fish jumped off the hook.

22. After we snooped around the office, we found the contract on a chair.

23. The excited boy reeled in his first fish, which was dangling from the fishhook by its mouth.

24. While the vultures were circling overhead, Jack watched them hovering nearby.

25. It started to rain while I was walking the dog around the block.

26. While Henry and Lynn were cleaning out the attic, they found an old family photograph album.

27. Their friends took them to an expensive, fancy new restaurant.

Unclear Pronoun Reference
Page 56
Sentences will vary. Following are examples of correct sentences.

1. Mrs. Hardin mentioned to Mrs. Mitchell that Mrs. Mitchell could begin decorating the table for the buffet.

2. When employees and supervisors discuss safety conditions, the workers report what they think are the dangerous areas in the plant.

3. With rain and snow, I find it hard to get around town.

4. Mr. Underling has been asking Jeremy to bring Jeremy's money for the trip.

5. Discussing the incident, the reporter said that Ms. West was not responsible for her behavior.

6. On a regular basis, that television station broadcasts news that is positive and enhances the community.

7. The Franklins invited some friends to the picnic, but the friends couldn't come.

Pronoun References in a Passage
Page 57
Paragraphs will vary slightly. Following is an example paragraph.

After studying 6,000 families, two researchers have listed the characteristics of strong families. In strong families, there is a sense of commitment to the family. Everyone knows that the family comes first. Work, friends, and possessions are second in importance to the family. People in strong family units appreciate each other and look at the positive strengths of each member. These families spend a great deal of time together doing things they like. Strong families cope well with crises and stress. They solve problems among them in constructive ways that increase family strength. Good communication in which adults and children talk to each other freely is another characteristic of strong families. Families become strong not by chance, but by design. By believing in each other and by working hard to build good relationships, every family can build its strength.

GED Practice: Sentence Structure
Pages 58–61

1. **(1) replace has with have** The plural verb have matches the subject devices.

2. **(3) disc player. "Universal"** Only option (3) corrects the run-on sentence.

3. **(4) signals which are** The plural verb are is needed to match signals, the plural antecedent of the pronoun which.

4. **(5) no correction is necessary** The sentence is correct as written.

5. **(4) replace them with it** The singular pronoun it is used to refer to the singular antecedent TV.

6. **(4) remotes are ready** Only option (4) uses the necessary plural, present tense verb.

7. **(2) replace it with them** The plural pronoun them is used to refer to the plural antecedent remotes.

8. **(4) replace don't with doesn't** The singular contraction doesn't is needed to match the singular subject task.

9. **(5) no correction is necessary.**

10. **(1) have extra functions and more** The sentence is correct as written.

11. **(4) replace them with they** The pronoun is the subject of the verb cost; therefore, they is the correct form.

12. **(4) replace whom with who** The subject pronoun who is needed to act as the subject in the clause who thinks so.

13. **(5) basis. According to** Only option (5) corrects the run-on sentence.

14. **(2) replace builds with build** The plural verb build matches the plural subject chemicals.

15. **(4) replace them with it** The singular pronoun it is used to refer to the singular antecedent manganese.

16. **(2) replace the comma with is** Only option (2) corrects the sentence fragment by adding a predicate.

17. **(2) remove the comma after sadness** Do not use a comma to set off a phrase that is necessary to the clarity of the sentence.

18. **(2) stop as soon as the** Only option (2) makes sense in this sentence.

19. **(4) replace stops with stop** The plural verb stop matches the plural subject tears.

20. **(2) replace most with more** Use more to compare two things (comparing people to others).

21. **(3) is** The rewritten sentence is "Crying under stress is a tendency that may be hereditary."

22. **(4) and cry it out** Only option (4) has a parallel structure to listen to your body.

23. **(5) no correction is necessary**

24. **(2) replace your with you're** The contraction you're is needed to provide both a subject and predicate for the sentence.

SIMULATED TEST A, PART I

Pages 62–74

1. **(4) change uses to use** (Usage-Subject/Verb Agreement) The subject appliances is plural and requires the plural verb use. In option (1), each would refer to one appliance. Option (3) is incorrect because a comma is needed prior to an interrupting phrase.

2. **(2) remove the comma after panels** (Mechanics/Punctuation) A comma is not used when a dependent clause follows the independent clause. Options (1) and (3) are singular verbs and do not agree with the plural subject (boards).

3. **(2) are manufactured** (Usage-Verb Tense) The paragraph is in present tense. Options (1) and (4) are in past tense; option (5) is in future tense; and option (3) does not match the plural subject.

4. **(5) When the boards** (Sentence Structure-Subordination) Option (5) shows the logical relationship between the two thoughts. Options (1) and (4) do not convey an appropriate relationship. Options (2) and (3) create run-on sentences.

5. **(2) replace commonest with common** (Usage-Comparative Adjectives) The -est endings are not used in combination with other superlative adjectives. Option (1) would not agree with the singular subject (cause).

6. **(4) remove here** (Usage-Conciseness) Here is an unnecessary word and is not correctly used in this sentence. Option (3) cannot be used since who always refers to people.

7. **(2) is being tested** (Usage-Subject/Verb Agreement) The singular verb is matches the singular subject (technology). Option (1) is plural. Options (3), (4), and (5) are in the wrong tense.

8. **(1) change the spelling of benifit to benefit** (Mechanics-Spelling) The correct spelling is benefit. In option (4), should be expresses an opinion that is not stated in the passage.

9. **(1) will** (Sentence Structure-Subordination) The rewritten sentence is: "Only scientists' creativity will limit the application of this technology." All other options do not make sense.

10. **(4) replace faster with fast** (Usage-Comparative Adjectives) Faster is an adjective used to compare two objects. Nothing is being compared in this sentence; therefore, the positive degree (fast) should be used. Option (1) does not match the plural subject (diets).

11. **(4) food is eaten, but** (Sentence Structure-Sentence Fragments) A helping verb must be used with the past participle eaten. Options (3) and (5) do not match the present tense of the sentence. Option (2) uses a plural verb instead of the required singular form.

12. **(1) insert a comma after day** (Mechanics-Punctuation) A comma must be used before and after an interrupting phrase. Option (2) is in the wrong tense, and option (3) cannot be used since helping verbs are present.

13. **(4) replace his with their** (Sentence Structure-Pronoun Agreement) The pronoun their agrees in number with the antecedent (patients). Option (1) is singular. Option (2) would be used if the sentence was talking about only one patient. Option (3) is incorrect because commas must be used to separate items in a list.

14. **(3) diets; for example, a typical program** (Sentence Structure-Subordination) The most effective sentence from the options is: "There are some serious drawbacks to these diets; for example a typical program costs at least $100 per week, bringing the total cost of the program to over $2,000." The other groups of words do not show a logical relationship.

15. **(5) no correction is necessary** (Mechanics-Comma Use) The sentence is correct as written. Option (1) is incorrect because it does not match the plural subject. Do not use a comma before a series of items.

16. **(1) replace them with these** (Usage-Pronoun Use) The correct pronoun is these. Option (2) is incorrect because a plural verb is needed. Option (4) needs a helping verb. A comma is not needed when the dependent clause follows the independent one.

17. **(3) replace them with dieters** (Sentence Structure-Unclear Pronoun Reference) In the original sentence, it is not clear to whom the word them refers. Dieters specifies who. A comma is needed after an introductory phrase. The plural verb phrase are encouraging matches the plural subject (programs).

18. **(4) program, a person** (Mechanics-Punctuation) When a dependent clause comes before an independent one, it must be set off with a comma. Option (2) produces a sentence fragment. Options (3) and (5) do not have logical connecting words. A semicolon cannot be used unless two independent clauses are being joined.

19. **(3) replace there with their** (Usage-Pronoun Use) The possessive pronoun their must be used to refer to individuals. No commas are needed in this sentence.

20. **(1) change the spelling of companys to companies** (Mechanics-Spelling) The correct plural of company is companies. Option (4) cannot be used since only two things are being compared. The comma after the dependent clause is needed since an independent clause follows it.

21. **(2) replace gets with get** (Usage-Subject/ Verb Agreement) The plural verb get must be used to match the plural subject (letters). Who cannot be used to refer to objects. Include matches the plural subject (letters).

22. **(4) and expresses your** (Sentence Structure-Parallel Structure) Only option (4) has a parallel structure to describes the problem.

23. **(4) you expect** (Usage-Verb Tense) The rest of the paragraph is written in present tense, so expect is the correct form. Options (1) and (2) are in past tense; option (3) is in future tense. Note the subject you always takes a plural verb, not a singular verb as indicated in option (5).

24. **(1) replace weather with whether** (Usage-Word Choice) Whether indicates a choice; weather refers to climate conditions. A comma is needed in a list of items. And does not indicate a choice. When the whether... or construction is used, the verb matches the subject closest to it. In this case, replacement is singular, so the singular verb form is used.

25. **(1) replace Its with It's** (Mechanics-Punctuation) The contractions It's must be used here since it contains the verb (It is your responsibility...). Always say each word in a contraction to determine if it contains a needed verb or if a possessive pronoun is appropriate in a sentence.

26. **(1) company, they may not feel** (Sentence Structure-Subordination) A comma is used to connect an introductory dependent clause to an independent clause. Options (2) and (5) create sentence fragments. Options (3) and (4) use semicolons incorrectly.

27. **(4) replace satisfies with satisfy** (Usage-Subject/Verb Agreement) The plural verb satisfy matches the plural subject they. Option (2) uses the wrong tense. The comma usage is correct.

28. **(3) request a** (Usage-Clarity) The rewritten sentence is: "In your closing statement, request a speedy resolution and state that you have included a proof of purchase." All other choices do not make sense.

29. **(4) Writing** (Usage-Subject Use) Writing is a gerund that introduces a gerund phrase used as a subject of this sentence. None of the other choices make sense.

30. **(1) remove who** (Sentence Structure-Sentence Fragments) By removing who, the original sentence fragment becomes a complete sentence: "Many people grow vegetable gardens to increase the quality of produce their families consume." The plural verb consume matches its subject (families).

31. **(4) gardening include the** (Sentence Structure-Subordination) The combined sentence is: "Other reasons people are attracted to backyard gardening include the convenience of having fresh vegetables close at hand and the savings accrued by growing their own food." The other choices do not make logical connections.

32. **(4) replace use with uses** (Usage-Subject/Verb Agreement) The singular verb uses matches the singular subject (family). Option 1 is in the wrong tense. Ones has to be used to refer to the plural antecedent (vegetables). A comma cannot be used to separate compound verbs.

33. **(3) does not take** (Usage-Verb Tense) Only option (3) is singular to match the subject and is in the present tense. Options (2), (4), and (5) are in the wrong tense.

34. **(3) replace their with his or her** (Sentence Structure-Pronoun/Antecedent Agreement) The singular pronoun his or her must be used to match its singular antecedent (dweller). No commas are needed in this sentence.

35. **(5) no correction is necessary** (Sentence Structure-Subordination) The sentence is correct as written.

36. **(4) replace Summer with summer** (Mechanics-Capitalization) The names of the seasons are not capitalized. The correct plural form of tomato is tomatoes.

37. **(5) will only produce a large harvest** (Sentence Structure-Misplaced Modifier) The adverb only should be placed as close to the verb phrase as possible to make the meaning of this sentence clear.

38. **(5) no correction is necessary** (Mechanics-Punctuation) The sentence is correct as written.

39. **(4) or canned** (Sentence Structure-Parallel Structure) Only option (4) is in parallel structure with the verb phrase can be frozen.

40. **(4) is the leading cause of** (Usage-Clarity) Option (4) is the only choice that makes sense in the sentence. Word order is important to convey clear meaning.

41. **(4) change the spelling of infecktion to infection** (Mechanics-Spelling) Infection is the correct spelling. Option (1) is the wrong tense. The comma after 1967 is needed to separate the dependent clause from the independent one that follows it.

42. **(1) old. Asian** (Sentence Structure-Subordination) Options (2), (3), (4), and (5) attempt to connect two unrelated sentences. Only option (1) keeps the ideas separated.

43. **(2) insert a comma after contagious** (Mechanics-Punctuation) A comma is needed before a short word that connects two independent but related thoughts. The possessive is not needed. The singular verb does matches the singular subject (illness), and the plural verb are matches its subject (scientists).

44. **(1) usually begin within** (Sentence Structure-Clarity) The rewritten sentence is: "The symptoms of Kawasaki Syndrome that children exhibit usually begin within one month of a carpet being cleaned in the home." The other choices do not clearly convey the meaning.

45. **(2) children, especially those under five,** (Mechanics-Punctuation) Commas are needed before and after an interrupting phrase.

46. **(2) are also advised** (Usage-Verb Tense) Only option (2) uses a present tense verb which is consistent with the verb tense used in the rest of the paragraph.

47. **(3) replace are with is** (Usage-Subject/Verb Agreement) The singular verb is matches the singular subject (virus). Do not use a comma to separate a subject from a verb.

48. **(2) replace increases with increase** (Usage-Subject/Verb Agreement) A plural verb is needed to match the compound subject (diagnosis and treatment). A comma is not used to separate two subjects.

49. **(3) when planning home improvement projects.** (Usage-Verb Tense) Options (1) and (2)

are not in the present tense. Options (4) and (5) do not have logical connecting words. Only option (3) makes sense in this sentence.

50. **(4) change the spelling of lisenced to licensed** (Mechanics-Spelling) Licensed is the correct spelling. Option (2) does not agree with the subject. The comma after bonded is needed since a list is given. Option (5) is incorrect because a comma should not be used after the last word in a list.

51. **(3) contractor and talk** (Sentence Structure-Sentence Fragments) Option (3) is the correct punctuation. Do not separate compound verbs (verify and talk) with a comma.

52. **(5) information and specify** (Sentence Structure-Parallel Structure) Options (1), (2), (3), and (4) do not have verb forms in parallel structure with the remainder of the sentence. The present tense verb form is needed (give, specify).

53. **(1) are usually included** (Usage-Subject/Verb Agreement) The rewritten sentence is: "Any warranties on the work performed or materials used are usually included in the contract." All other options contain singular verb forms that do not match the plural subject (warranties).

54. **(3) Taking time to think over** (Usage-Subordination) The rewritten sentence is: "Taking time to think over a contract is a way to avoid high-pressure sales tactics." The other word groups do not make sense.

55. **(5) no correction is necessary** (Usage-Verb Tense) This sentence is correct as written.

Simulated Test A, Part II
Page 75

Follow the Essay correction instructions on page 108.

Following is a sample essay that supports a ban on handguns. This essay was scored 5.

Handguns should be banned in America for three basic reasons. Many children are killed accidentally when they innocently play with guns. The number of people who are killed by relatives would decrease if guns were not so readily available. Violent crime may be reduced if criminals had more difficulty in obtaining guns.

Children who find a handgun often think it is a harmless toy. Being curious, they examine the gun. As a result, many children accidentally shoot their brothers, sisters, or friends. If guns were banned, it would reduce the number of guns that are carelessly left in places where children can find them.

If guns were banned, there would not be so many domestic murders. When a woman is arguing with her husband, for example, she may pick up a gun and shoot him without really thinking about the consequences.

Criminals are the primary users of handguns. While committing a crime such as robbery, criminals use guns to make it easier for them to prey on innocent victims. Many people might be saved if criminals were not able to purchase handguns.

Many accidental deaths occur because handguns are left unattended or are used in the heat of passion. They are used when crimes are committed, and there do not

seem to be any advantages for citizens to continue to allow guns to be sold. Everyone should support a law to ban handguns in the United States.

(approximately 237 words)

Following is a sample essay that opposes a ban on handguns. This essay was scored 5.

Handguns are necessary to protect citizens' property and lives from criminals. Our right to defend ourselves is guaranteed in the Bill of Rights. If guns were banned, only criminals would have access to them, and law-abiding citizens would be left defenseless.

The black market in guns would significantly increase if handguns were banned. This would make it easy for criminals to obtain guns, but difficult for people who may be the victims of crime.

Every citizen has the right to defend his or her property and the lives of their family. Banning handguns would be a violation of this right. If a criminal enters a person's home with the intent to rob a family, that family needs access to a gun to defend themselves.

Target shooting using handguns is enjoyed by many people as a sport. The skills of marksmanship are taught and valued by many citizens. There are shooting ranges where law-abiding people can enjoy this sport.

Banning guns would not solve the problem of crime, but it would leave citizens without a means to defend themselves. In addition, a sport that is currently legal would be made illegal. Citizens throughout the country should oppose a ban on handguns because a ban would be unconstitutional.

(approximately 208 words)

SIMULATED TEST B, PART I
Pages 77–89

1. **(1) change the spelling of emergancy to emergency** (Mechanics-Spelling) Emergency is the correct spelling. The plural verb treat matches the plural subject staffs. A comma is not needed. Children and who are correctly used.

2. **(5) no correction is necessary** (Sentence Structure-Parallel Structure) The sentence is correct as written.

3. **(2) the hospital, the** (Mechanics-Punctuation) When a dependent clause comes before an independent clause, use a comma, not a semicolon. Options (3) and (5) do not use logical connecting words.

4. **(5) is** (Sentence Structure-Clarity) The rewritten sentence is: "Remaining calm is important to be able to make appropriate decisions regarding your child's care." The other choices do not clearly convey the meaning.

5. **(3) replace them with parents** (Usage-Pronoun Antecedent) Parents makes the meaning of the pronoun clear. Commas are not needed after often or children. The plural verb encourage matches the plural subject hospitals.

6. **(2) Although you are anxious, you** (Sentence Structure-Subordination) Only the word although indicates the proper relationship between the two clauses.

7. **(4) situations; for example, if** (Usage-Logical Relationships) The combined sentence is: "Kids take cues from their parents on how to react to situations; for example, if you're hysterical, your child may become more frightened from your reaction than from his or her actual discomfort." For example conveys the relationship between the two clauses.

8. **(4) replace them with him or her** (Usage-Pronouns) Them is a plural pronoun that incorrectly refers to a singular antecedent child. In is the proper connecting word. No semicolon is needed. Is matches the singular subject what.

9. **(4) remove more** (Usage-Comparative Adjectives) More is used to compare two or more objects or ideas and is unnecessary in this sentence. Your is a possessive pronoun that shows to whom the participation belongs. No comma is needed. Treat matches its plural subject staff. Safely is parallel to quickly.

10. **(1) injured, but** (Usage-Verb Use) The original sentence uses the correct verb structure and shows the proper relationship between the two clauses.

11. **(2) replace and with or** (Sentence Structure-Subordination) Or is needed to indicate the choice after whether. The comma after yard is needed for a list of items. The comma after balcony separates the dependent clause from the independent one that follows it. The present tense verb is matches the tense of the passage.

12. **(3) fish, vegetables, and breads** (Sentence Structure-Parallel Structure) Only option (3) is in parallel structure. All other choices are not parallel.

13. **(4) wood; in fact, the** (Sentence Structure-Subordination) The combined sentence is: "The wonderful smoky barbecue flavor can be enhanced by adding different kinds of wood; in fact, the most popular are mesquite and hickory." None of the other connecting words shows the appropriate relationship.

14. **(3) replace it with them** (Usage-Pronoun Use) It refers to a plural antecedent (wood chunks, chips) and thus needs the plural form them. Before expresses the right time to soak the chips. The comma is necessary to separate the dependent clause from the independent one that follows it. No comma is needed after water.

15. **(1) grapevines and herbs that lend** (Usage-Verb Use) The sentence is correct as written. None of the other options is in parallel structure and have the needed verb form.

16. **(2) replace its with it's** (Mechanics-Punctuation) The contraction it's is needed. Have matches the plural subject grills. No other commas are needed.

17. **(2) smoke if meats are** (Usage-Verb Use) Only option (2) has correct punctuation and has a plural verb to match the subject meats.

18. **(4) breads should be grilled over** (Sentence Structure-Sentence Fragments) Option (4) supplies the necessary verb form.

19. **(5) replace centurys with centuries** (Mechanics-Spelling) The correct plural form of century is centuries. No commas are needed in this sentence. Is matches the singular subject meal.

20. **(2) insert is after popcorn** (Sentence Structure-Sentence Fragments) Only option (2) provides a singular verb to match the subject popcorn.

21. **(1) in Chicago, Americans buy** (Sentence Structure-Sentence Fragments) The combined sentence is: "According to the Popcorn Institute located in Chicago, Americans buy over 800 million pounds of unpopped popcorn each year." The other choices do not clearly convey the meaning.

22. **(1) replace Brothers with brothers** (Mechanics-Capitalization) Brothers does not need to be capitalized. No commas are needed in this sentence. Have matches the plural subject brothers.

23. **(3) has been started** (Usage-Subject/Verb Agreement) Only option (3) supplies the necessary singular verb form.

24. **(1) replace are with is** (Usage-Subject/Verb Agreement) Is matches the singular subject ear. The comma after oven separates two clauses. The comma after white separates two adjectives. There is no verb bursted.

25. **(4) The kernels stay** (Usage-Pronoun Use) Kernels is needed to replace the ambiguous pronoun they. The other two options that use kernel as the subject do not indicate an appropriate relationship between the two clauses.

26. **(1) replace enjoys with enjoy** (Usage-Subject/Verb Agreement) The plural subject people requires the plural verb enjoy. No comma is needed. The possessive pronoun their is needed to show ownership of eyes.

27. **(3) has captivated kids wherever** (Sentence Structure-Verb Tense) Only option (3) expresses the correct verb tense and number. Wherever is needed since it is referring to a place, not a time.

28. **(4) remove the comma after red** (Mechanics-Punctuation) Do not separate the last of a list of items from the rest of the sentence. The possessive form of brothers is not needed. Are matches the plural subject.

29. **(5) no correction is necessary** (Sentence Structure-Sentence Combining) The sentence is correct as written.

30. **(1) replace You're with Your** (Usage-Word Choice) The possessive pronoun your is needed, not a contraction. Needs matches the singular subject. The comma after dirt is needed to separate items in a list.

31. **(2) change the spelling of convenient to convenient** (Mechanics-Spelling) Convenient is the correct spelling. Are matches the plural subject. The comma after convenient is needed to connect two independent clauses. No other commas are needed. The possessive form car's is needed to describe whose finish.

32. **(3) enough water, the** (Mechanics-Punctuation) Only option (3) correctly punctuates a dependent clause followed by an independent one and also shows the correct relationship.

33. **(3) if** (Sentence Structure-Clarity) The rewritten sentence is: "Since most car washes recycle their water, if the water isn't properly filtered, salt and dirt could be deposited back on your car." The other choices do not clearly convey the meaning.

34. **(4) Car washes that use** (Usage-Pronoun Use) Only option (4) clearly states the subject car washes and uses an appropriate verb structure.

35. **(5) no correction is necessary** (Sentence Structure-Parallel Structure) The sentence is correct as written.

36. **(2) driven, but the** (Sentence Structure-Subordination) The combined sentence is: "The hot wax treatment makes the water bead up on the car's finish, which prevents streaking as the car is driven, but the wax only lasts for a week at most." The other choices do not clearly convey the meaning.

37. **(3) insert a comma after time-consuming** (Mechanics-Punctuation) A comma is needed after consuming to separate an unnecessary clause. The comma after Hand-washing is needed to separate the clause as well. The contraction it's is needed because it contains the verb is. Is matches the singular subject it.

38. **(4) wash, however, should** (Mechanics-Punctuation) Only option (4) uses correct punctuation. In this sentence, however is an interrupting word, not a conjunction.

39. **(3) replace mend with mended** (Usage-Verb Use) Mended is needed in the verb phrase. The comma after glue is needed to separate an interrupting phrase from the rest of the sentence. Has matches the singular subject glue. No comma is needed.

40. **(4) glue is being used to** (Usage-Verb Use) Only option (4) uses the correct verb tense.

41. **(1) remove the comma after stitches** (Mechanics-Punctuation) No comma is needed after stitches because the dependent clause follows the independent one. No other commas are needed. There is no reason to use the possessive form of scar. To leave would be incorrect.

42. **(2) to avoid scars** (Sentence Structure-Clarity) To avoid is used as an infinitive. All other options include verbs that are not needed.

43. **(5) completely if a cut** (Sentence Structure-Conciseness) Sentences should be concise. When and if are not necessary. All other choices are too wordy or do not contain a conjunction that makes sense in this sentence.

44. **(2) replace allow with allows** (Usage-Subject/Verb Agreement) The singular verb allows is needed to match the singular subject glue. The comma after cuts is needed to separate the introductory phrase from the rest of the sentence. No other commas are needed. Forms is needed to match its singular subject tissue.

45. **(5) face, tissue glue is** (Usage-Pronoun Use) Only option (5) specifies what it is, and uses a correct verb form. Options (3) and (4) would form questions.

46. **(3) also reduces** (Usage-Verb Tense) Only option (3) expresses the present tense that is used in the rest of the passage.

47. **(3) replace lie with lay** (Sentence Structure-Word Choice) Lay, meaning to place or set down, is needed in this sentence. The comma is needed to separate an interrupting phrase. Are matches the plural subject physicians. They're is a contraction of they are, which would not make sense in this sentence.

48. **(3) life may be taking** (Usage-Verb Tense) Only Option (3) is in present tense, which matches the rest of the passage.

49. **(3) replace Doctors with doctors** (Mechanics-Capitalization) In this sentence, doctors is a common noun that does not need to be capitalized. No commas are needed. Because would be incomplete without of.

50. **(5) replace most with more** (Usage-Comparative Adjectives) More is used to compare two things (stress and your reaction). Until would not express the appropriate relationship of the dependent clause. Is matches its singular subject stress. The comma is needed to join the dependent clause to the rest of the sentence. Affects is the needed verb form.

51. **(2) ignored, thereby depleting** (Sentence Structure-Subordination) The combined sentence is: "When you're under stress, good eating habits are often ignored, thereby depleting your body of essential nutrients." The other choices do not clearly convey the meaning of the sentence.

52. **(4) replace their with your** (Usage-Pronoun Use) The entire passage uses the form your. Makes matches the singular subject stress. Speed matches its subject hormones.

53. **(1) replace Scientist's with Scientists** (Mechanics-Punctuation) The plural noun scientists is used as the subject of the sentence. Are is present tense and plural to match the subject. Is is singular to match its subject relaxation. No commas are needed.

54. **(2) and breathing rates** (Sentence Structure-Parallel Structure) Only option (2) puts the two elements (heart rate and breathing rate) in a parallel form.

55. **(4) feel more energetic** (Sentence Structure-Parallel Structure) Only option (4) uses a structure that is parallel to lower your stress level.

Simulated Test B, Part II
Page 90

Follow the Essay correction instructions on page 108.

Following is a sample essay for Part II. This essay was scored 5.

Children can be well cared for whether they stay at home daily or go to a day-care center. The experiences are different, but each type has benefits and weaknesses. The differences relate to the parent/child relationship, the type of activities provided, and the amount of interaction with other children.

A parent who stays at home to care for his or her children is usually available to immediately comfort a child who has fallen. At a day-care center, someone will comfort the child, but it won't be the parent. The difference in the type of relationship established between a parent and child is based in part on the parent being available to see about the child's needs.

At a day-care center, children have the opportunity to play with many types of toys. At home, children have a limited choice of toys. Children at day-care centers often take field trips to a zoo or museum. They have more organized activities than most children who stay at home.

Children at day-care centers socialize with a greater number of other people than do children who stay at home. Many children who are cared for at home often spend a great deal of time alone or with family members. For this reason, children who attend day-care centers may be more social, initially, than children who are raised at home.

Whether a child goes to a day-care center or stays at home daily, both can have positive experiences. The type of parent/child relationship, the activities in which the child engages, and the number of social contacts the child makes are generally different.

Essay Evaluation Instructions

GED test scorers will evaluate your essay holistically—by judging its overall effectiveness. To the scorers, how clearly you present your ideas is the most important thing. A few misspelled words or a few errors in grammar will not cause your essay to receive a low score, although too many of these errors might. The GED Essay Scoring Guide that follows tells what characteristics essay scorers use when they read an essay.

GED Essay Scoring Guide

Copyright © 1987, GED Testing Service

Papers will show *some or all* of the following characteristics.

Upper-half papers have a clear, definite purpose pursued with varying degrees of effectiveness. They have a structure that shows evidence of some deliberate planning. The writer's control of the conventions of Standard Written English (spelling, punctuation, grammar, word choice, and sentence structure) ranges from fairly reliable at 4 to confident and accomplished at 6.

6   The *6 paper* offers sophisticated ideas within an organizational framework that is clear and appropriate for the topic. The supporting statements are particularly effective because of their substance, specificity, or illustrative quality. The writing is vivid and precise, although it may contain an occasional error in the conventions of Standard Written English.

5   The *5 paper* is clearly organized with effective support for each of the writer's major points. While the writing offers substantive ideas, it lacks the fluency found in the 6 paper. Although there are some errors, the conventions of Standard English are consistently under control.

4   The *4 paper* shows evidence of the writer's organizational plan. Support, though adequate, tends to be less extensive or effective than that found in the 5 paper. The writer generally observes the conventions of Standard Written English. The errors that are present are not severe enough to interfere significantly with the writer's main purpose.

Lower-half papers either fail to convey a purpose sufficiently or lack one entirely. Consequently, their structure ranges from rudimentary at 3, to random at 2, to absent at 1. Control of the conventions of Standard Written English tends to follow this same gradient.

3   The *3 paper* usually shows some evidence of planning, although the development is insufficient. The supporting statements may be limited to a listing or a repetition of ideas. The 3 paper often demonstrates repeated weaknesses in the conventions of Standard Written English.

2   The *2 paper* is characterized by a marked lack of organization or inadequate support for ideas. The development is usually superficial or unfocused. Errors in the conventions of Standard Written English may seriously interfere with the overall effectiveness of this paper.

1   The *1 paper* lacks purpose or development. The dominant feature is the absence of control of structure or the conventions of Standard Written English. The deficiencies are so severe that the writer's ideas are difficult or impossible to understand.

*   An asterisk code is reserved for papers that are blank, illegible, or written on a topic other than the one assigned. Because these papers cannot be scored, a Writing Skills Test composite score cannot be reported.

Reprinted with permission of the American Council on Education.

For your essays, have your teacher evaluate your essays if you are taking a class. If you are working independently, ask a friend or relative to read your essays. If this is not possible, evaluate your writing yourself. After finishing an essay, put it aside for a day. Then read it as objectively as possible. No matter who checks your writing, make sure that person uses the chart on this page as a guide.

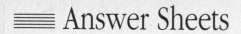
Answer Sheets

GED Writing Skills, Part I

Name: _____ Class: _____ Date: _____

1 ① ② ③ ④ ⑤   11 ① ② ③ ④ ⑤   21 ① ② ③ ④ ⑤   31 ① ② ③ ④ ⑤   41 ① ② ③ ④ ⑤   51 ① ② ③ ④ ⑤

2 ① ② ③ ④ ⑤   12 ① ② ③ ④ ⑤   22 ① ② ③ ④ ⑤   32 ① ② ③ ④ ⑤   42 ① ② ③ ④ ⑤   52 ① ② ③ ④ ⑤

3 ① ② ③ ④ ⑤   13 ① ② ③ ④ ⑤   23 ① ② ③ ④ ⑤   33 ① ② ③ ④ ⑤   43 ① ② ③ ④ ⑤   53 ① ② ③ ④ ⑤

4 ① ② ③ ④ ⑤   14 ① ② ③ ④ ⑤   24 ① ② ③ ④ ⑤   34 ① ② ③ ④ ⑤   44 ① ② ③ ④ ⑤   54 ① ② ③ ④ ⑤

5 ① ② ③ ④ ⑤   15 ① ② ③ ④ ⑤   25 ① ② ③ ④ ⑤   35 ① ② ③ ④ ⑤   45 ① ② ③ ④ ⑤   55 ① ② ③ ④ ⑤

6 ① ② ③ ④ ⑤   16 ① ② ③ ④ ⑤   26 ① ② ③ ④ ⑤   36 ① ② ③ ④ ⑤   46 ① ② ③ ④ ⑤

7 ① ② ③ ④ ⑤   17 ① ② ③ ④ ⑤   27 ① ② ③ ④ ⑤   37 ① ② ③ ④ ⑤   47 ① ② ③ ④ ⑤

8 ① ② ③ ④ ⑤   18 ① ② ③ ④ ⑤   28 ① ② ③ ④ ⑤   38 ① ② ③ ④ ⑤   48 ① ② ③ ④ ⑤

9 ① ② ③ ④ ⑤   19 ① ② ③ ④ ⑤   29 ① ② ③ ④ ⑤   39 ① ② ③ ④ ⑤   49 ① ② ③ ④ ⑤

10 ① ② ③ ④ ⑤   20 ① ② ③ ④ ⑤   30 ① ② ③ ④ ⑤   40 ① ② ③ ④ ⑤   50 ① ② ③ ④ ⑤

Name: _____ Class: _____ Date: _____

_____

_____

_____

_____

_____

_____

_____

_____

_____

_____

_____

_____

_____

_____

_____

_____

_____

_____

_____

_____

_____

Continue your essay on your own paper.

USE A BALL POINT PEN TO WRITE YOUR ESSAY